WIMBLEDON
- 2022 -

CENTRE COURT
100

WIMBLEDON
- 2022 -

CENTRE COURT
100

By Paul Newman
& Alix Ramsay

Published in 2022 for the All England Lawn Tennis Club by Vision Sports Publishing

Vision Sports Publishing Ltd
19-23 High Street
Kingston upon Thames
Surrey
KT1 1LL
www.visionsp.co.uk

ISBN: 978–1913412–39–5

Written by: Paul Newman and Alix Ramsay
Edited by: Jim Drewett and Alexandra Willis
Photographic manager: Bob Martin
Assistant editor: William Giles
Production editor: Ed Davis
Picture research: Sarah Frandsen
Photographic reproduction: Bill Greenwood
Proofreading: Lee Goodall

All photographs © AELTC unless otherwise stated

Photographers and editors:
Bob Martin, Thomas Lovelock, Simon Bruty, Jed Leicester, Florian Eisele, Ben Solomon,
David Gray, Eddie Keogh, Ian Walton, Jonathan Nackstrand, Jed Jacobson, Adam Warner,
Edward Whitaker, Chloe Knott, Jon Super, Sammie Thompson, Neil Turner, Richard Ward,
Joe Toth, Ben Queenborough, Ian Roman, Dillon Bryden, Anne Schwarz, Andrew Baker,
James Smith, Karwai Tang, Anthony Upton, Felix Diemer, Lucy Bull, Sean Ryan, Kieran Cleeves
Mike Lawrence

Results and tables are reproduced courtesy of the AELTC

The All England Lawn Tennis Club (Championships) Limited
Church Road
Wimbledon
London
SW19 5AE
England
Tel: +44 (0)20 8944 1066
www.wimbledon.com

Printed in Slovakia by Neografia

This book is published with the assistance of Rolex

CONTENTS

—

Top: An aerial shot of the Grounds in their centenary year taken from a helicopter during The Championships 2022

Above: Gentlemen's Singles Champion Novak Djokovic and Ladies' Singles Champion Elena Rybakina pose with the famous trophies before the Champions' Dinner

FOREWORD

—

By Chairman Ian Hewitt

Welcome to this special edition of the Wimbledon Annual.

It was 100 years ago that the All England Club moved to a new ground off Church Road. The instruction went out from Commander Hillyard, the Club Secretary, "Let us construct and equip our ground so that it is immediately recognised not only as the finest in England but in the world." And so, 100 years since King George and Queen Mary took their seats in the Royal Box to watch the opening of play on Centre Court (it duly rained…), we welcomed players, guests, and fans back to that same stadium, to witness another chapter in the history of Wimbledon. The Stage Awaits.

Not only was it a first full capacity Championships since 2019, it was also one of significant change. The first year of a 14-day schedule with play on the Middle Sunday, the first year of a 14&U draw in the Junior Championships, the first year of a new central entrance to Centre Court, the return of the Queue and Ticket Resale, and a wide variety of improvements and innovations.

We were also proud to host the return of so many great Wimbledon champions to Centre Court for our celebration on the Middle Sunday. From Roger Federer to Angela Mortimer, it was a privilege to witness.

But it was the tennis, as it should, that grabbed the headlines. From Serena Williams' return, to Andy Murray and Emma Raducanu's earlier exits, to Cameron Norrie, and of course Nick Kyrgios, we saw epic triumphs and enthralling upsets. The final act crowned a new champion, as Elena Rybakina claimed her maiden Wimbledon title, alongside a well-known one – Novak Djokovic securing his fourth consecutive title, and seventh overall. Congratulations to all.

Finally, I would like to thank everyone involved in the organisation and staging of The Championships this year. The stewards, the officials, Ball Boys and Girls and those who train them, the catering staff, the ground staff, the security staff, all the executive team, and so many others, and of course the players – the principal actors on our stage.

I. L. Hewitt

ROGER FEDERER

GARBIÑE MUGURUZA

BJÖRN BORG

WHAT IS SO SPECIAL?

What is so special about this place? Beyond its history as the oldest tennis tournament in the world? Beyond its atmosphere and its rituals, summer drizzles, strawberries and cream, all a hop, skip and a jump from Central London? Beyond its unique colours, pristine white and vibrant green? And for that matter, beyond the grass, painstakingly cut to a sharp 8mm every single morning? And above all, beyond the epic matches that were disputed on it, and still are? Games that have pushed standards far beyond their discipline. Standards to play by. Standards to live by. This is the place where tennis legends are written. **Welcome to Wimbledon.**

#Perpetual

OYSTER PERPETUAL
DATEJUST 41

CENTRE COURT
100

THE CHAMPIONSHIPS, WIMBLEDON
THE ALL ENGLAND LAWN TENNIS CLUB,
LONDON 27 JUNE TO 10 JULY 2022

ROLEX

INTRODUCTION

—

By Paul Newman

The coronavirus pandemic has taught us all that 'normality' can never be taken for granted, but as The Championships 2022 approached there could be no mistaking the sense of anticipation among all those for whom Wimbledon holds a special place in their hearts.

Two years after the cancellation of The Championships as Covid swept the globe, and 12 months after its return in front of limited crowds, the most cherished event in world tennis would finally be taking place again without restrictions. For the first time since 2019 there would be no limits on spectator numbers other than the return to a Grounds capacity of 42,000; the Queue would return; and there would be no need for players, officials or the public to undergo mandatory Covid testing.

There were other reasons, too, to expect The Championships 2022 to take place in a celebratory mood. It was exactly 100 years since the All England Lawn Tennis & Croquet Club had moved from its original home in Worple Road on the other side of Wimbledon to its current Church Road site: time, therefore, to celebrate the centenary of Centre Court at Church Road, the essential character of which had remained unchanged ever since Algernon Kingscote and Leslie Godfree contested the very first match in the stadium in front of King George V in 1922. It would also be a time for Wimbledon to join the country's celebration of The Queen's Platinum Jubilee and to mark the 100th birthday of the BBC, which has been broadcasting from The Championships ever since 1927, just five years after its inception.

While The Championships 2022 would offer the chance to look back on some glorious history, the All England Club had also spent much of the previous 12 months looking forward to the next 100 years. Time never stands still at Wimbledon, where innovation and tradition walk hand in hand.

Perhaps the most significant change would be the introduction of scheduled play on Middle Sunday for the first time in the 145-year history of The Championships. Although there had been play on

HISTORIC FIRST

Practice makes perfect – even for the courts. For the first time the players were invited to practice on Centre and No.1 Courts before The Championships started. This 'played in' the courts and left them in prime condition for the opening day. *Clockwise from above:* Serena Williams, Emma Raducanu (who had just come to get a feel for the atmosphere before her opening match), Coco Gauff, Novak Djokovic and Rafael Nadal all took full advantage of the opportunity – ably assisted by the Ball Boys and Girls.

Middle Sunday on four previous occasions to deal with a backlog of matches caused by bad weather, this would be the first time that The Championships had been scheduled as a 14-day event. The change was made in order to make more matches accessible to more people, both at home and overseas, and to build more resilience into the programme for the players. It was also hoped that Middle Sunday would develop an identity of its own, particularly through a focus on the local community.

Playing on Middle Sunday led to significant changes to the programme in the second week. All gentlemen's and ladies' fourth round singles matches had previously been scheduled for the first day of the second week on what had become known as 'Manic Monday'. Now, half of those matches would be moved to Middle Sunday. There would also be changes to the second Tuesday and Wednesday, which would both feature two gentlemen's quarter-finals and two ladies' quarter-finals. The final of the mixed doubles would now be played on the second Thursday, to give it greater profile, while the ladies' doubles final would become the concluding match on the last Sunday.

The extra day's play also enabled some competitions to be expanded. The Quad Wheelchair draws had been doubled in size and the Junior Championships extended to include a new competition for players aged 14 and under. The Invitation events would return for the first time in three years, with the events repurposed to feature a mixed doubles competition alongside the ladies' and gentlemen's doubles draws.

The 'Central Reveal' – the new player entrance to Centre Court, positioned just below the Royal Box

Centre Court had a new central entrance for players, while eagle-eyed observers might notice a new balustrade around the Royal Box and the court's surrounds, in keeping with the stadium's original 1922 design by Captain Stanley Peach. A new umpire's chair would be in use on Centre Court and No.1 Court, while all match officials would be wearing new outfits produced by Ralph Lauren, the Official

Outfitter of The Championships. All honours boards on the site had been updated: 'Miss' or 'Mrs' had been removed from the names of female competitors, while married champions were recorded by their own names rather than those of their husbands. Meanwhile umpires would be calling all players by their first and second names: the new world No.1, for example, would be referred to as 'Iga Swiatek' rather than 'Miss Swiatek'.

For the first time, first-to-10-points tie-breaks would be introduced at 6-6 in the final sets of all matches in Qualifying, gentlemen's and ladies' singles and doubles, Wheelchair and junior singles competitions. Until this year the Grand Slam events had each used different formats to settle matches that went the distance, but the Grand Slam Board had now agreed, initially on an experimental basis, to use the same system in all four competitions to provide greater consistency. It was an example of a reinforced spirit of co-operation between the four organisations, whose chief executives congregated in person at the All England Club in the week before The Championships for the first time since before the pandemic.

That week was also a significant one for Centre Court, as players were able to practise in the stadium for the first time. After Serena Williams and Adrian Mannarino had suffered match-ending injuries on the second day last year following falls on the lush surface, it was hoped that having players practise on the court in the build-up to the start of competition would help to bed the court in more quickly.

Williams had not played in the ensuing 11 months, but the former world No.1 had accepted a wild card into The Championships. Rafael Nadal, who had won the first two Grand Slam events of the year, would also be coming, having recovered from the foot injury he had exacerbated in winning his 14th Roland-Garros title. However, Venus Williams, who had been absent from the court for

The updated ladies' singles honours board gets a last-minute polish

2008   V. Williams
2009   S. Williams
2010   S. Williams
2011   P. Kvitova
2012   S. Williams
2013   M. Bartoli
2014   P. Kvitova
2015   S. Williams
2016   S. Williams
2017   G. Muguruza
2018   A. Kerber
2019   S. Halep
2021   A. Barty

ALL SMILES AT THE ALL ENGLAND

No more Covid restrictions, no more player bubbles – Wimbledon was back to normal and everyone was loving it. *Clockwise from left:* Andy Murray returns from practice, Emma Raducanu warms up without her racket and Storm Sanders is at full stretch. *Opposite, clockwise from top:* Novak Djokovic shares a joke (or, possibly, a 'Djoke') with Ajla Tomljanovic; Serena Williams, Iga Swiatek, Nick Kyrgios, Cameron Norrie and Simona Halep were in cheery mood in their media conferences; while Denis Shapovalov (*centre*) was all smiles on the practice courts.

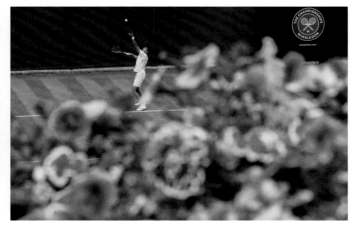

the previous 10 months, would be missing from the singles draws, as would Roger Federer, Ashleigh Barty, Alexander Zverev and Naomi Osaka. Federer was still recovering from the knee surgery he had undergone after The Championships 2021, Barty had retired (at the age of just 25) eight months after winning the ladies' singles and Zverev and Osaka were out with ankle and Achilles injuries respectively.

The other notable absentees were all Russian and Belarusian players, including Daniil Medvedev, the world No.1, Aryna Sabalenka, a semi-finalist in 2021, and Victoria Azarenka, a former Grand Slam champion. Following Russia's invasion of Ukraine in February, the All England Club Board had decided, following Government guidance and "with deep regret", to decline entries from Russian and Belarusian players because it would have been "unacceptable for the Russian regime to derive any benefits from the involvement of Russian or Belarusian players". As a consequence, the Association of Tennis Professionals and Women's Tennis Association had announced that no ranking points would be given to players competing at The Championships.

The removal of ranking points initially prompted suggestions that some players might boycott The Championships, but in the end almost everybody who was fit and eligible to play arrived in SW19. Increased prize money, which was up 11.1 per cent on 2021, might have been a factor for a handful of players, but for the vast majority the prospect of opting out of the sport's most celebrated and revered competition was simply unthinkable.

Opposite: The 42 acres of the Grounds are decorated with more than 50,000 plants, all carefully nurtured to come into full bloom for the start of the Fortnight

Below: Pick a racket, any racket – Rafael Nadal certainly has plenty to choose from

GENTLEMEN'S SINGLES SEEDS

—

1

Novak DJOKOVIC
(Serbia)
Age: 35
Wimbledon titles: 6
Grand Slam titles: 20

2

Rafael NADAL
(Spain)
Age: 36
Wimbledon titles: 2
Grand Slam titles: 22

3

Casper RUUD
(Norway)
Age: 23
Wimbledon titles: 0
Grand Slam titles: 0

4
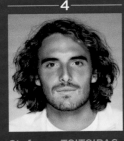

Stefanos TSITSIPAS
(Greece)
Age: 23
Wimbledon titles: 0
Grand Slam titles: 0

5
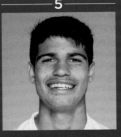

Carlos ALCARAZ
(Spain)
Age: 19
Wimbledon titles: 0
Grand Slam titles: 0

6

Felix AUGER-ALIASSIME
(Canada)
Age: 21
Wimbledon titles: 0
Grand Slam titles: 0

7

Hubert HURKACZ
(Poland)
Age: 25
Wimbledon titles: 0
Grand Slam titles: 0

8

Matteo BERRETTINI
(Italy)
Age: 26
Wimbledon titles: 0
Grand Slam titles: 0

9

Cameron NORRIE
(Great Britain)
Age: 26
Wimbledon titles: 0
Grand Slam titles: 0

10

Jannik SINNER
(Italy)
Age: 20
Wimbledon titles: 0
Grand Slam titles: 0

11
Taylor
FRITZ
(USA)

12
Diego
SCHWARTZMAN
(Argentina)

13
Denis
SHAPOVALOV
(Canada)

14
Marin
CILIC
(Croatia)

15
Reilly
OPELKA
(USA)

16
Pablo
CARREÑO BUSTA
(Spain)

17
Roberto
BAUTISTA AGUT
(Spain)

18
Grigor
DIMITROV
(Bulgaria)

19
Gael
MONFILS
(France)

20
Alex
DE MINAUR
(Australia)

21
John
ISNER
(USA)

22
Botic
VAN DE
ZANDSCHULP
(Netherlands)

23
Nikoloz
BASILASHVILI
(Georgia)

24
Frances
TIAFOE
(USA)

25
Holger
RUNE
(Denmark)

26
Miomir
KECMANOVIC
(Serbia)

27
Filip
KRAJINOVIC
(Serbia)

28
Lorenzo
SONEGO
(Italy)

29
Daniel
EVANS
(Great Britain)

30
Jenson
BROOKSBY
(Spain)

LADIES' SINGLES SEEDS

—

1

Iga SWIATEK
(Poland)
Age: 21
Wimbledon titles: 0
Grand Slam titles: 2

2

Anett KONTAVEIT
(Estonia)
Age: 26
Wimbledon titles: 0
Grand Slam titles: 0

3

Ons JABEUR
(Tunisia)
Age: 27
Wimbledon titles: 0
Grand Slam titles: 0

4

Paula BADOSA
(Spain)
Age: 24
Wimbledon titles: 0
Grand Slam titles: 0

5

Maria SAKKARI
(Greece)
Age: 26
Wimbledon titles: 0
Grand Slam titles: 0

6

Karolina PLISKOVA
(Czech Republic)
Age: 30
Wimbledon titles: 0
Grand Slam titles: 0

7

Danielle COLLINS
(USA)
Age: 28
Wimbledon titles: 0
Grand Slam titles: 0

8

Jessica PEGULA
(USA)
Age: 28
Wimbledon titles: 0
Grand Slam titles: 0

9

Garbiñe MUGURUZA
(Spain)
Age: 28
Wimbledon titles: 1
Grand Slam titles: 2

10

Emma RADUCANU
(Great Britain)
Age: 19
Wimbledon titles: 0
Grand Slam titles: 1

11
Coco **GAUFF**
(USA)

12
Jelena **OSTAPENKO**
(Latvia)

13
Barbora **KREJCIKOVA**
(Czech Republic)

14
Belinda **BENCIC**
(Switzerland)

15
Angelique **KERBER**
(Germany)

16
Simona **HALEP**
(Romania)

17
Elena **RYBAKINA**
(Kazakhstan)

18
Jil **TEICHMANN**
(Switzerland)

19
Madison **KEYS**
(USA)

20
Amanda **ANISIMOVA**
(USA)

21
Camila **GIORGI**
(Italy)

22
Martina **TREVISAN**
(Italy)

23
Beatriz **HADDAD MAIA**
(Brazil)

24
Elise **MERTENS**
(Belgium)

25
Petra **KVITOVA**
(Czech Republic)

26
Sorana **CIRSTEA**
(Romania)

27
Yulia **PUTINTSEVA**
(Kazakhstan)

28
Alison **RISKE-AMRITRAJ**
(USA)

29
Anhelina **KALININA**
(Ukraine)

30
Shelby **ROGERS**
(USA)

31
Kaia **KANEPI**
(Estonia)

32
Sara **SORRIBES TORMO**
(Spain)

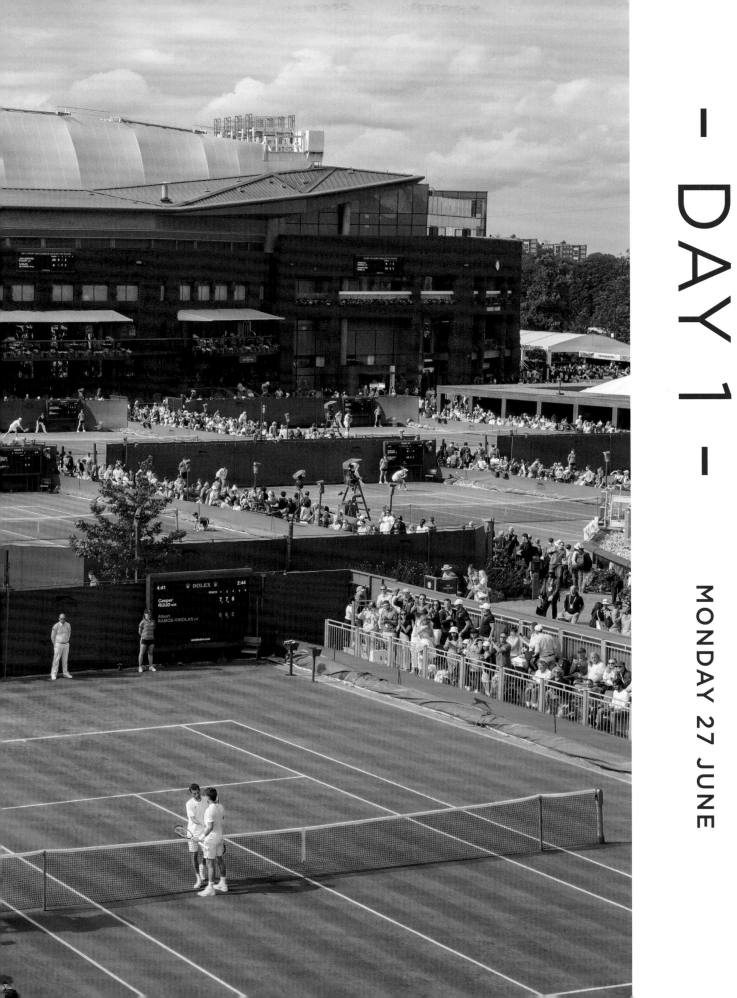

THE ALL ENGLAND LAWN TENNIS & CROQUET CLUB

I t was no wonder that Novak Djokovic savoured what he called the "unique and special feeling" of playing the opening match on Centre Court as defending champion. Beating South Korea's Soonwoo Kwon 6-3, 3-6, 6-3, 6-4 was the perfect way to leave behind some of the difficult moments the 35-year-old Serb had faced in the 50 weeks since he had lifted the Gentlemen's Singles Trophy at The Championships for the sixth time the previous summer.

Above: His stage awaits – Novak Djokovic walks through the new entrance to Centre Court to begin the defence of his gentlemen's singles title

Previous pages: Packed walkways, all seats filled and action on every court – this is Wimbledon at its best

After that triumph Djokovic had headed for the US Open, with the aim of becoming the first man since Rod Laver in 1969 to achieve a pure calendar-year Grand Slam of the sport's four biggest trophies. Winning the first three in 2021 had left Djokovic equal with Roger Federer and Rafael Nadal on a total of 20 Grand Slam singles titles. With Federer injured and Nadal having not added to his tally since Roland-Garros 2020, the then world No.1 was in prime position to settle all arguments about who was the greatest male singles player of all time.

At Flushing Meadows, however, Djokovic faltered, losing in straight sets to Daniil Medvedev in the final. Much worse was to follow in the opening weeks of 2022. Djokovic had chosen to remain unvaccinated against Covid despite entry rules into Australia requiring all players to have had their injections, but after contracting the virus in December he was led to believe that he would be allowed to play at the Australian Open. On his arrival in Melbourne, however, Djokovic was detained by immigration authorities, who said he did not meet federal coronavirus requirements. After 10 days of

wrangling, during which time he was detained in an immigration detention hotel, he was deported the day before the Australian Open started.

Unable to enter the United States in the spring for the same reason, Djokovic had played only one tournament by the start of the European clay court season, though he soon rediscovered his form, winning the title in Rome. At Roland-Garros, however, he lost to Nadal in the quarter-finals. With Nadal going on to win the title, having also triumphed at the Australian Open in January, the Spaniard went into The Championships with 22 Grand Slams to his name, two more than Djokovic.

Given some of the hostile reactions Djokovic had faced because of his vaccination stance, particularly in Australia, the Serb was unsure what sort of reception he would receive when he stepped on to Centre Court to face Kwon. The crowd's reaction was less effusive than might have been expected for the return of a six-times champion, but Djokovic was happy. "I was very pleasantly surprised, in a positive way," he said afterwards. "Of course, the crowd was engaged in the match. They supported both players. I thought they were very fair to me."

As he had done so often in the past, Djokovic arrived at the All England Club without any competitive grass court matches under his belt. There was clearly some rustiness in his game, but his victory over the world No.81, which started under a closed roof because of rain, was never in serious doubt. With his victory Djokovic became the only man to have won 80 or more singles matches at each of the four Grand Slam events. "I did not play at my best, but I think when I needed to find the right shots, I did," he said afterwards. "For the first match I'm pleased."

For anyone with Centre Court tickets, and those watching on television in the UK, it was a day to relish as the following two matches featured returning British heroes in the shape of Emma Raducanu and Andy Murray. Raducanu's extraordinary 2021 season, highlighted by her stunning triumph at

Soonwoo Kwon, the world No.81, acknowledges the applause from the Royal Box before he takes on one of the toughest challenges in tennis – Novak Djokovic on Centre Court

the US Open, had taken off at last year's Championships, when she won three matches on her Grand Slam debut, just weeks after finishing her A-level exams. At Flushing Meadows, where she was still ranked only No.150 in the world, the then 18-year-old Briton went on one of the most remarkable runs in tennis history, winning 10 matches in a row without dropping a set. She became the first British woman to win a Grand Slam title since Virginia Wade in 1977 and the first qualifier to win a Grand Slam title in the Open era.

However, the following months had not been easy. In the 13 tournaments Raducanu had played since New York, she had made only one quarter-final. Some observers felt that frequent changes in her coaching staff were not helping, while others questioned how she was coping with her new-found fame. Her progress had also been hampered by injury setbacks; in her only warm-up tournament on grass she had retired hurt in her opening match with a side strain.

For her Centre Court debut Raducanu faced the world No.46, Alison Van Uytvanck, who had won two lower-level grass court titles in the preceding weeks and had knocked out the defending champion, Garbiñe Muguruza, four years earlier. Raducanu struggled to deal with the 28-year-old Belgian's variations of pace in the opening stages but soon got on top and went on to win 6-4, 6-4, despite going 3-1 down in the second set.

Raducanu came into her post-match press conference wearing a t-shirt featuring Rafael Nadal's bull horns logo. "Rafa just embodies fight, that sort of energy," she said. "That's what I'm bringing in. Energy-wise, I've had a tough year. It's no secret. It's all worth it just to go out on Centre Court and get a win like that. I definitely am very happy to be here. All the lessons I've taken from the last year will only hold me in good stead for the future."

Murray had been through torrid times since suffering a serious injury in 2017, but after undergoing major hip resurfacing surgery and coming through several subsequent setbacks his fortunes had taken a turn for the better in the last year. In January he had reached the final of a tournament in Sydney and in June, after choosing to miss Roland-Garros, he reached his first grass court final since his 2016 Wimbledon triumph. Stefanos Tsitsipas and Nick Kyrgios were among his victims in Stuttgart before Matteo Berrettini denied him the title.

Murray, who had brought Ivan Lendl back for a third spell as his coach, missed the Queen's Club tournament because of an abdominal injury, but looked in good shape as he maintained his record of never losing in the first round at The Championships by beating James Duckworth 4-6, 6-3, 6-2, 6-4. After a slow start, the 35-year-old Scot's growing confidence was underlined when he threw in an underarm serve. "I don't know how many more opportunities I'll get to play on this court, so I want to make the most of every time I get to come out here," he said to the crowd afterwards.

Opposite: After a rollercoaster 12 months since she was last at Wimbledon – a period that saw her win the US Open but only 10 matches thereafter – Emma Raducanu celebrates victory over Alison Van Uytvanck

RIGHT ON QUEUE

At 2pm precisely on the eve of The Championships, the Queue officially began. Missing since 2019 due to Covid restrictions, this iconic part of Wimbledon was back in all its glory. The stalwarts camp overnight, hoping to be able to buy one of the limited number of tickets to Centre, No.1 and No.2 Courts that are available. Those who arrive later wait for Grounds Passes. But they all make the experience almost as much of an occasion as the tennis. Special mention must go to Brandt Pham (*left*), who took no chances and arrived two days early at 6pm on the Friday before finally claiming his prize – a Centre Court ticket on Monday (*opposite, bottom*).

Cameron Norrie had recorded the first British victory of The Championships, beating Pablo Andujar 6-0, 7-6(3), 6-3 on No.2 Court despite two rain breaks. The first home player to go out, Jodie Burrage, was beaten 2-6, 3-6 by Ukraine's Lesia Tsurenko, who admitted afterwards that she found it difficult to focus on her tennis while bombs were falling near her home in Kyiv. "For me emotionally winning or losing doesn't exist any more," she said. "For me, there is one big issue in my life: it's war." Her next opponent would be her fellow countrywoman, Anhelina Kalinina, who said she would use her prize money to help rebuild her parents' home after it was bombed during the Russian invasion.

Poland's Hubert Hurkacz, a semi-finalist 12 months earlier, was the most significant loser on the opening day as the No.7 seed was beaten 6-7(4), 4-6, 7-5, 6-2, 6-7(8) by Alejandro Davidovich Fokina. The Spaniard recovered his composure in the tie-break at the end of the deciding set, having failed to convert three match points when serving at 5-3 in the third set. Pablo Carreño Busta, the No.16 seed, retired hurt at one set apiece in his encounter with Dusan Lajovic, while Marin Cilic's campaign ended before he had struck a ball as the 2017 runner-up fell victim to Covid.

Casper Ruud, who had made huge strides in the last year to reach the world's top 10, finally recorded his first victory at The Championships at the third attempt, beating Albert Ramos-Vinolas 7-6(1),

Hip-hip-hooray! Andy Murray celebrates after his four-set win over James Duckworth. The former champion, now down to No.52 in the rankings, was arguably playing his best tennis since undergoing hip resurfacing surgery in 2019

CELEBRATING WITH A NEW LOOK

—

It was not only the Centre Court that had a new look for its centenary celebration – the umpires, line judges and Ball Boys and Girls all had a makeover, too. Polo Ralph Lauren, the official outfitter of The Championships, had designed new uniforms for them all.

The umpires had new belted-back sportscoats lined with a commemorative Wimbledon print accented with both Ralph Lauren and Championships logos, which was paired with a wide Bengal stripe shirt and white trousers or skirts. The line judges sported navy cardigans featuring a white and Wimbledon green-striped cuff detail, while the Ball Boys and Girls wore the famous Ralph Lauren polo shirt in a broad blue and white stripe.

The outfits were made of sustainable, innovative fabrics, some made from recycled materials and all manufactured to standards that consider both communities and the environment.

7-6(9), 6-2. Carlos Alcaraz, another rising force, needed five sets to beat Jan-Lennard Struff, while Stan Wawrinka, who had returned to competition after a long absence following foot surgery, lost in four sets to Jannik Sinner, who claimed his first Tour-level victory on grass. John Isner returned to Court 18, the scene of his epic 11-hour victory over Nicolas Mahut 12 years earlier, and was drawn into another five-set marathon, but beat Enzo Couacaud after three and a quarter hours.

Anett Kontaveit, seeded No.2 after winning five titles since her last visit to The Championships, beat Bernarda Pera, while the No.3 seed, Ons Jabeur, celebrated her rise to No.2 in the world that day by beating Mirjam Bjorklund. Angelique Kerber, the 2018 champion, beat Kristina Mladenovic, but Danielle Collins, the No.7 seed and runner-up at the Australian Open, lost to Marie Bouzkova. An arguably bigger surprise was Kaja Juvan's victory over Beatriz Haddad Maia, the No.23 seed, who had just won grass court titles at both Nottingham and Edgbaston. On the biggest stages, sometimes even the best preparation is not enough.

Anett Kontaveit leans into another backhand on her way to victory against Bernarda Pera in the first round on No.2 Court

DAILY DIARY DAY 1

Booing at Wimbledon? Surely not. Yet there was a distinct booing noise coming from Court 12 as Casper Ruud (*above*), the Roland-Garros runner-up, faced Albert Ramos-Vinolas. Fear not, the crowd had not forgotten their manners; they were just cheering for the Norwegian by chanting his name over and again: "Ruuuuuud! Ruuuuuud!" Although it sounds like a boo, Casper has heard it many times before; he knew they were on his side. And he won, too.

• Getting to know the new neighbours is always a tricky business – you want to make a good impression, but you also want to lay down a few ground rules ('That's my front garden and not a parking spot for your bins...'). Cameron Norrie found this out when, as the No.9 seed, he moved into the Gentlemen's Members' Dressing Room for the first time (that is the locker room within the Centre Court complex reserved for the top seeds). His locker was next to Novak Djokovic's – and it seemed that the defending champion was not the tidiest of neighbours. "I was asking him how Centre Court was, talking to him a little bit," Cam said of their first encounter. "Mostly all his stuff was in the way of mine. I was trying to get past him, trying to get to my locker!"

• You just never know when a Percy Pig is going to come in handy (other confectionary products are also available...). Jodie Burrage (*right*) was doing her best to find a way past Lesia Tsurenko on Court 18 when she

spotted a Ball Boy looking wobbly at the start of the second set. Rushing to his aid, she offered him an energy drink and gel. "He just said he was feeling really faint," she explained. Having felt faint herself on court in the past, Burrage knew exactly what she was dealing with. "I was just like: 'This kid needs sugar'," she said. "He wasn't liking the gel. They're not the nicest things to have, so I said: 'We definitely need something else'. Someone just shouted on the side: 'Got some sweets here if you want!'. They were Percy Pigs. Percy Pigs are one of my favourites. So I definitely recommend it if it ever happens again." Sadly for Jodie, she could not revive her chances of reaching the second round and lost in straight sets.

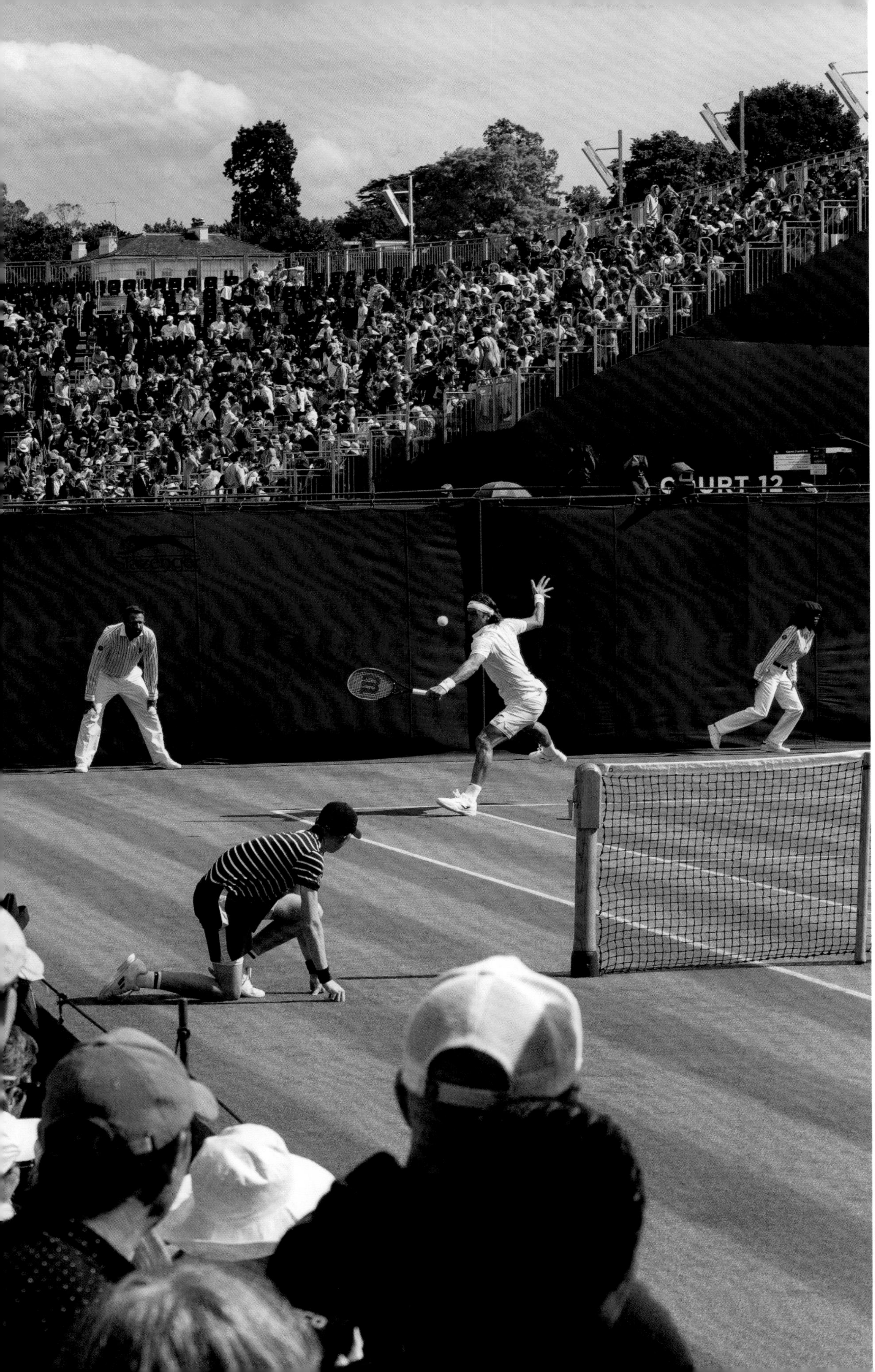

– DAY 2 –

TUESDAY 28 JUNE

It was one of the enduring images of The Championships 2021: a tearful Serena Williams, her right leg heavily strapped, hobbling out of Centre Court, having retired hurt in her opening match against Aliaksandra Sasnovich. As she limped off, the seven-times Ladies' Singles Champion had taken time to wave to all corners of the stadium in a manner that left us wondering whether this might be her final farewell.

Above: The look in Serena Williams' eye when she won the second set seemed like the Serena of old but Harmony Tan kept the former champion on the back foot

Previous pages: Feliciano Lopez plays possibly his last match at Wimbledon on Court 4, losing to Botic van de Zandschulp

Over the next 11 months the likelihood of Williams playing again seemed to diminish with each passing day. In August she withdrew from the US Open, citing the hamstring she had torn at Wimbledon, in September she turned 40, and in December she pulled out of the Australian Open, despite earlier indications that she might return there. When Patrick Mouratoglou, her coach since 2012, announced in April that he would be working with Simona Halep, it seemed only a matter of time before the 23-times Grand Slam singles champion would confirm her retirement.

Williams, nevertheless, has spent a professional lifetime confounding expectations and in June came news that even her most diehard fans might have feared they would never hear. Eleven months after her last appearance on a court, she would be playing as a wild card at Eastbourne and Wimbledon – intending to play doubles with Ons Jabeur on the coast, and then singles at SW19. Although the Eastbourne adventure ended after two matches when Jabeur pulled out with a knee injury, Williams, had done enough to suggest that she could still be a factor at The Championships, 24 years after her first Wimbledon appearance.

The Wimbledon draw offered some encouragement as Williams was paired with Harmony Tan, a 24-year-old Frenchwoman ranked No.115 in the world. Tan was making her debut at The Championships and had won only two matches in her six previous appearances at Grand Slam tournaments.

At the start of their evening encounter on Centre Court, however, it was Williams whose form reflected her ranking, the former No.1 having dropped to No.1,204 in the world due to her inactivity. Failing to find her timing on her ground strokes, Williams went 0-2 down, recovered to lead 4-2 but eventually lost the 64-minute opening set 5-7. With Tan slowing the rallies down with drop shots and slices, Williams struggled to create her own pace. As Simon Briggs wrote in *The Daily Telegraph*, "the impression was of a dinghy sailing rings around a stately galleon, staying out of the way of the heavy cannon while inflicting numerous minor wounds".

With darkness drawing in, the Centre Court roof was closed, after which the volume of noise from a boisterous crowd rose as the momentum shifted. Williams won a game of 12 deuces to go 2-0 up in the second set, which she went on to win 6-1. By the time she led 3-1 in the deciding set it seemed the crisis might be over, but Williams failed to serve out for victory at 5-4 and had to save a match point two games later. In the deciding tie-break Williams took a 4-0 lead, only for Tan to fight back. After three hours and 11 minutes and with the 11pm curfew less than 25 minutes away, Williams missed a forehand when 7-9 down, handing Tan a dramatic 7-5, 1-6, 7-6(7) victory.

"I'm so emotional now," Tan said in her on-court interview afterwards. "Serena is a superstar and when I was young I was watching her so many times on the TV. For my first Wimbledon, it's wow. Just wow. When I saw the draw I was really scared, because it's Serena Williams, she's a legend. I thought if I could win one or two games it was really good for me."

Williams, who had lost in a Grand Slam first round singles on only two previous occasions, said she had given everything but had paid for her lack of "match toughness". Asked whether this might be her

No one looked more stunned than Harmony Tan after her victory over seven-times champion Serena Williams

last match, she replied: "That's a question I can't answer. I don't know. Who knows where I'll pop up?" Nevertheless, the experience had clearly reignited her competitive fires and she talked as if this might not be her parting shot. "It definitely makes me want to hit the practice courts," she said.

The second day's Centre Court programme is usually opened by the defending Ladies' Singles Champion, but Ashleigh Barty had shocked the sport in March by announcing her retirement. Instead the honour fell to Iga Swiatek, who had stepped into Barty's shoes as world No.1 and was on a remarkable 35-match winning run. After the Roland-Garros champion had brushed aside Croatia's Jana Fett for the loss of only three games, she was asked what it felt like to have put together a longer unbeaten run than Serena or Venus Williams had ever achieved. "When I see Serena or see Venus, they seem like the legends," she said. "I don't consider myself a legend."

Halep and Petra Kvitova, two former champions, came through their opening tests in contrasting styles. Halep needed only 65 minutes to beat Karolina Muchova 6-3, 6-2 in her first match at The Championships since her 2019 triumph, but Kvitova had to recover from a shaky start before beating Jasmine Paolini 2-6, 6-4, 6-2. The champion of 2011 and 2014 had won the fifth grass court singles title of her career at Eastbourne only three days earlier and said she had struggled to handle the different conditions at the All England Club. She put her victory over Paolini down to her "fighting spirit".

Coco Gauff, who had just played in her first Grand Slam final at Roland-Garros, also had to dig deep in her opening match, recovering to beat the world No.54, Elena-Gabriela Ruse, 2-6, 6-3, 7-5 after two hours and 29 minutes. Elena Rybakina, the No.17 seed, beat Coco Vandeweghe, twice a quarter-finalist here, 7-6(2), 7-5 in a tight encounter that would fortify her for some of the battles ahead.

Felix Auger-Aliassime, a quarter-finalist in 2021, became the highest seed in the gentlemen's singles to go out when he lost 7-6(5), 4-6, 6-7(9), 6-7(5) to Maxime Cressy, a serve-and-volley specialist, after more than four hours. The No.6 seed praised his American opponent's courage. "His serve was amazing," Auger-Aliassime said. "He took his chances when he needed to in important points."

For the second day in a row a former Wimbledon runner-up pulled out as Matteo Berrettini, the beaten finalist in 2021, announced that, like Marin Cilic, he had tested positive for Covid. Auger-Aliassime, Berrettini and Cilic had been in the same half of the draw as Rafael Nadal, who beat the

world No.41, Francisco Cerundolo, 6-4, 6-3, 3-6, 6-4 in his first match at The Championships for three years. Nadal, who had won at Roland-Garros for the 14th time in his last competitive appearance three weeks earlier, said his victory over Cerundolo had been "very positive", though he still had plenty of room for improvement. Stefanos Tsitsipas, who had gone out in the first round in his two previous appearances at The Championships, beat Alexander Ritschard, who was making his Grand Slam debut, 7-6(1), 6-3, 5-7, 6-4.

Controversy is never far away when Nick Kyrgios is on court and the 27-year-old Australian once again found himself the focus of attention in his 3-6, 6-1, 7-5, 6-7(3), 7-5 victory over Paul Jubb, a 22-year-old Briton finding his way on the Tour after a successful college tennis career in the United States. Playing with renewed confidence following recent victories over James Duckworth and Steve Johnson in qualifying at Queen's, Jubb kept Kyrgios on court for more than three hours.

Coco Gauff recovered from a nervy start against Elena-Gabriela Ruse to reach the second round

THE VERY BEST OF BRITISH

—

By Day Two, and for the first time since 1997, Britain had nine players in the second round of the singles.

Cameron Norrie started proceedings on the opening day, closely followed by Emma Raducanu and Andy Murray. On Tuesday, Ryan Peniston, Jack Draper, Katie Boulter, Heather Watson, Alastair Gray and Liam Broady had joined them, while Paul Jubb – raised by his grandmother, Valerie, on a council estate in Hull – narrowly missed out on joining them, losing in five sets to Nick Kyrgios. The following day saw Harriet Dart boost the contingent to 10. Each of these players were obviously delighted, but perhaps none so much as Peniston. Diagnosed with a rare soft tissue cancer as a baby, he was a late bloomer and had never played a main Tour match until the 2022 grass court season but impressed everyone with quarter-final finishes at Queen's and Eastbourne before registering his first Wimbledon win.

Broady credits this success to the Battle of the Brits events organised by Jamie Murray in 2020 and 2021 – which brought British players together to train and compete and gave the lower-ranked players a chance to learn from their more experienced compatriots. Training with the LTA now follows the same pattern: everyone practises with everyone.

"Andy [Murray] and Jack Draper will have great practices," Broady said. "Whereas when I was 18, I was just practicing with other 18-year-olds."

Clockwise from top left: Ryan Peniston, Alastair Gray, Liam Broady, Cameron Norrie, Emma Raducanu, Andy Murray, Katie Boulter and Jack

Draper. Opposite page: Heather Watson celebrates (top), while Paul Jubb shakes hands with Nick Kyrgios (left)

Maxime Cressy on the move during his impressive victory over Felix Auger-Aliassime, the No.6 seed

Kyrgios became involved in a number of confrontations with spectators on No.3 Court, angered by what he saw as their lack of respect. At one stage he complained to the umpire: "You don't accept a hat with two logos on but you accept disrespect of an athlete?" Kyrgios described one line judge who had reported him to the umpire as "a snitch" and was particularly unhappy with one line call in the opening set. "Most of the umpires are older and I just don't think that's ideal when you're playing a sport of such small margins," he said afterwards. "Factually people that are younger have better eyesight." Kyrgios admitted afterwards that he had spat in the direction of a spectator who had been heckling him, an incident for which he was later fined $10,000.

Despite Jubb's defeat, it was generally a good day for British players. Ryan Peniston, who had made a big breakthrough by reaching the quarter-finals of four grass court tournaments in the build-up, beat Henri Laaksonen 6-4, 6-3, 6-2 on his Grand Slam debut. Having overcome a rare cancer as a baby which affected his growth as a teenager, 26-year-old Peniston said that his experiences had made him "tougher as a player and a person".

Jack Draper, Liam Broady, Alastair Gray and Katie Boulter all won their first round matches, as did Heather Watson, who completed a 6-7(7), 7-5, 6-2 victory over Tamara Korpatsch, their match having fallen victim to the 11pm curfew on No.1 Court the previous evening. Dan Evans, nevertheless, suffered a surprising defeat at the hands of Australia's Jason Kubler, the world No.99. At least the British No.2 kept his sense of humour. Asked if he felt he was missing out on the home players' party, Evans replied: "No, no. I can have a party on my own."

DAILY DIARY **DAY 2**

Novak Djokovic must have signed thousands of autographs in his life, but never once has he asked one of his fellow superstars to do the honours for his children, seven-year-old Stefan and four-year-old Tara. Until, that is, he spotted Venus Williams at the All England Club. Armed with a book and pen each, the children were introduced to the former champion by their proud dad. She duly signed for Tara who, with a little prompting from her father, shyly said thank you and shook Venus' hand – and then immediately turned her attention to see what Venus was now signing in Stefan's book. Well, you can't let your brother get a bigger autograph than you, can you?

• Obviously, in professional sport, winning matters. But not always. Zoe Hives (*left*) earned her ticket into the main draw by coming through the Qualifying Competition – and she could not quite believe that she had done it. She only returned to the Tour in January after two years spent dealing with postural orthostatic tachycardia syndrome, a condition so debilitating that, at times, she did not have the energy to walk the length of her driveway. But the draw pitted her against Maria Sakkari, the No.5 seed, and her Wimbledon was over in two sets. Still, she did receive a £50,000 prize money cheque which she thinks she may use to buy a new car. The Australian is often seen driving around her home town of Ballarat in a Hyundai that has seen better days, one that she shares with her mother. "But at least if I had a nicer car, she could use that instead," Zoe said. Sometimes, even losing can have an upside.

• At 40 years young, Feliciano Lopez was convinced that this, his 20th Wimbledon, was to be his last. His singles ranking had dipped to No.240 and trying to get back into the top 100 to ensure direct entry into any of the four Grand Slam tournaments seemed like too big a mountain to climb. And anyway, he had a busy life away from the match courts: he is a husband, a father and also the tournament director of the Madrid Open. As he said: "I will have plenty of things to do." But you can't keep a good man down; no sooner had he hung up his Wimbledon racket after his first round defeat at the hands of Botic van de Zandschulp than he had moved into the co-commentator's chair for the BBC and was calling some of Rafael Nadal's matches.

— DAY 3 —

WEDNESDAY 29 JUNE

A ndy Murray had been criticised by some in his earlier days for his demeanour, but for five years now the former world No.1's actions had spoken only of his optimism and positivity. It was hard to believe that anyone else would have kept going through the pain and anguish that the 35-year-old Scot had endured ever since he limped out of The Championships 2017 with a serious injury that eventually required major surgery.

Yet here he was, after his 4-6, 6-7(4), 7-6(3), 4-6 second round defeat to John Isner, talking positively about the future. "I really want to try and improve my ranking to a level where I'm getting seeded in Slams," Murray said after suffering his earliest-ever loss at The Championships. "I want to try and put myself in that position, hopefully come the US Open. If not the US Open, then going into the Australian Open next year. That means I'll need to be out there competing and winning matches, because it does make things trickier. I was coming into Wimbledon feeling like I could have a deep run. If you're playing against top guys right at the beginning of the event, it obviously makes it a little bit more challenging. That's what my goals are between now and the US Open."

When Murray finally decided to undergo hip resurfacing surgery at the start of 2019 he knew that it might spell the end of his career, but the two-times Gentlemen's Singles Champion threw himself into his rehabilitation programme with all his customary zeal. No player with a metal hip had ever gone on to play top-level singles again, but within nine months Murray had claimed the 46th title of

Andy Murray congratulates John Isner on his win. It was the Scot's earliest ever defeat at The Championships

his career in Antwerp. A number of physical setbacks interrupted his progress in the next two years, but by June 2022 Murray had clawed his way back into the world's top 50 for the first time since the summer of 2018.

Murray's latest problem had been an abdominal strain which had hampered his Wimbledon preparations, but he still had good reason to fancy his chances against Isner, a player he had beaten in all eight of their previous meetings. However, the 6ft 10in American has a huge serve – perhaps the best the sport has ever seen – and is always a formidable opponent on grass. Isner hit 38 aces as Murray won just 15 of the 94 points when the No.20 seed's first serve found its target. Thumping 82 winners to Murray's 39, Isner played well at crucial moments, converting two of his three break points while Murray failed to take either of his two. "It's one of those matches that, had I got through, who knows what would have happened," Murray said afterwards. However, he was pleased to have emerged without any more physical issues considering it had been "touch and go" the previous week as to whether he would have been fit to play at the All England Club.

Asked if he expected to be back at The Championships next year, Murray was cautious. "It's extremely difficult with the problems I've had with my body in the last few years to make long-term predictions about how I'm going to be even in a few weeks' time, never mind in a year's time," he said. "If I'm in a good place physically, yes, I will continue to play. But it's not easy to keep my body in optimal condition to compete at the highest level."

Isner paid credit to his opponent. "I am most definitely not a better tennis player than Andy Murray, but I might have just been a little better than him today," the 37-year-old American said. "It was an incredible honour to play him on this court in front of this crowd. At the age I'm at now, I need to relish these moments. This was one of the biggest wins of my career. To play as well as I did against one of our greatest players ever was a huge accomplishment for me. He's a massive inspiration to each one of us in the locker room and we are so lucky to still have him around."

Murray's defeat was the second successive loss for a home player on Centre Court after Emma Raducanu was beaten 3-6, 3-6 by Caroline Garcia. The 28-year-old Frenchwoman was ranked No.55 in the world, but her title triumph on grass at Bad Homburg the previous week had marked her out as a dangerous opponent. Garcia, a former top 10 player, went on the attack from the start and Raducanu was unable to counter her opponent's firepower. After her third second round defeat in a row at a Grand Slam event, Raducanu said that she needed to focus on her fitness, a side strain having limited her court time in preparation for The Championships. "I've played seven hours of tennis in a month," she said afterwards. "To even compete with these girls at this level and win a round I think is a pretty good achievement."

The US Open champion rejected suggestions that the pressures of being a Grand Slam champion had been weighing her down. "There's no pressure," she said. "Why is there any pressure? I'm still 19." She added: "Yes, I have had attention. But I'm a Slam champion, so no one's going to take that away from me. If anything, the pressure is on those who haven't done that."

Harriet Dart, a 6-1, 6-4 winner over Rebeka Masarova, took the number of British players through to the second round in singles to 10, the most at Wimbledon for 38 years. Ryan Peniston's campaign ended with a second round defeat to Steve Johnson, but Cameron Norrie became the first home player through to the last 32 when he beat his former doubles partner, Jaume Munar, 6-4, 3-6, 5-7, 6-0, 6-2. Heather Watson was on the brink of joining Norrie in the third round only for bad light to stop her match

IN SUPPORT OF UKRAINE

—

On the day that Lesia Tsurenko (*below, left*) beat Anhelina Kalinina, it was not the result that mattered, although Tsurenko won. It was the support both Ukrainian women felt from the whole of Wimbledon that meant the most.

The All England Club had relaxed its dress code to allow all players to wear ribbons in the Ukraine colours (Iga Swiatek (*above, left*) wore hers on her cap) and Tsurenko promised to send 10 per cent of her prize money back home to help those who had lost everything (Tsurenko's fitness coach is from Kremenchuk, where a shopping mall had been bombed the week before The Championships).

Refugees from the war who had found homes in the Wimbledon area were invited to a tea party before The Championships (*above*) and were given tickets to Centre Court for the Middle Sunday.

On the opening day Vadym Prystaiko, the Ukraine ambassador to the UK, had been a guest of Ian Hewitt, the Chairman of the AELTC (*right*).

"We felt amazing support, for sure," Tsurenko said.

when she was leading Qiang Wang 7-5, 5-4, the schedule on Court 18 having been held up earlier in the day because of rain. It was the second round in a row that Watson would have to come back the following day to complete her match.

Anett Kontaveit became the highest seed so far to go out of the competition when she was beaten 4-6, 0-6 in just 58 minutes by Jule Niemeier, a 22-year-old German playing in only her second Grand Slam event. The No.2 seed said afterwards that she was still struggling with the after-effects of Covid, which she had contracted two months earlier. Garbiñe Muguruza, the No.9 seed, also lost, winning just seven points in the second set of a 4-6, 0-6 defeat to Greet Minnen. However, there were no such problems for the five other top 15 seeds in action in the ladies' singles, with Ons Jabeur, Maria Sakkari, Jessica Pegula, Jelena Ostapenko and Angelique Kerber all winning in straight sets.

The day's biggest casualty in the gentlemen's singles was Casper Ruud. The No.3 seed was beaten 6-3, 2-6, 5-7, 4-6 by France's Ugo Humbert, the world No.112, who had lost in the first round in his five previous Grand Slam appearances. Novak Djokovic, who had looked in patchy form in his opening match, went through the gears against Thanasi Kokkinakis, beating the Australian 6-1, 6-4, 6-2 in just two hours. "I'm quite pleased with the way that I raised the level of tennis in two days," Djokovic said afterwards. "Hopefully, I can keep that trajectory, keep getting better as the tournament progresses. I'm obviously just thinking about the next challenge and hopefully things will get better and better."

Above: Harriet Dart on her way to a straight-sets victory over Rebeka Masarova – she was now the 10th Briton through to the second round

Opposite: Frances Tiafoe's serve was in full flow against Germany's Maximilian Marterer as he sped into the third round

57

Carlos Alcaraz, playing only the fourth match of his career on grass, also showed marked improvement on his first round performance in beating Tallon Griekspoor 6-4, 7-6(0), 6-3. The 19-year-old Spaniard, the youngest player in the gentlemen's singles field, had chosen not to play any warm-up events on grass following an excellent clay court season, during which he had won the titles in Barcelona and Madrid before reaching the quarter-finals at Roland-Garros. "I felt more comfortable today than I did in the first round, but obviously I need more hours on court, on grass, to feel more comfortable," he said.

The gentlemen's and ladies' doubles competitions got under way, but the most significant doubles news of the day was the announcement that Venus Williams would be playing in the mixed doubles event alongside Jamie Murray, the American and the Scot having been awarded a wild card. It would be her first appearance on a court since the previous August and would mean that both Murray brothers would have enjoyed the experience playing alongside a Williams sister at Wimbledon, Andy having joined forces with Serena in the mixed doubles in 2019.

Britain's Arthur Fery and Felix Gill are all smiles after they beat Ariel Behar from Uruguay and Gonzalo Escobar from Ecuador in the first round of the gentlemen's doubles on Court 11

DAILY DIARY DAY 3

Hydration drinks? Check. Snacks and power bars? Check. Almost entirely white kit? Check. Grass court shoes? Check. Game plan? Check. Right, we are ready to go. And off Ugo Humbert (*above*) went to No.2 Court for his appointment with Casper Ruud. It was only when he got there that he discovered that he had forgotten the most important item on his checklist: his rackets. No matter, once he had got over his embarrassment and had been reunited with the tools of his trade, he proceeded to dismiss the No.3 seed in four sets.

• Everyone is familiar with the Wimbledon rain delays, but a bee delay? That is a new one. Up on the roof of the Broadcast Centre, a swarm of bees had stopped for

a breather and were settling in nicely on a floral display when they were spotted by a member of the IBM data analysts team. Not that there was any cause for panic; the powers behind the scenes at the All England Club have everything covered and before anyone could say 'buzz' a beekeeper had been summoned to collect the insects and take them away safely. This perhaps may become a common occurrence during The Championships – as part of Wimbledon's Environment Positive aim, the variety and number of plants around the Grounds has been increased and that is what probably attracted the bees in the first place. As for the bees themselves, they missed a trick – if they had wanted a lie down they could have gone to the 'bug hotel'. Yes, Wimbledon has one of those, too.

• And it had all been going so well. Alejandro Davidovich Fokina had played his heart out on the opening day to beat Hubert Hurkacz – the No.7 seed and a semi-finalist last year – 10-8 in the fifth-set tie-break. He was on top of the world. Then he took on Jiri Vesely and, again, battled to a fifth set tie-break. But this time, when he lost a point to go 9-7 down in that decider, he had a sudden rush of blood to the head, thwacked the ball out of the court and was promptly docked a penalty point. The match was over and he was on his way home. Vesely had won without having to play another shot.

British tennis insiders had long known of Katie Boulter's talent and potential. Born into a tennis-loving family in Leicester, she had demonstrated her ball-striking ability from her earliest days on the court. At the age of five she had won the very first tournament she entered, competing against players up to five years older than her. At 18 she broke into the world's top 100, only to fall ill weeks later with a virus that soon developed into chronic fatigue syndrome.

It left the teenager exhausted even after going for a short walk, kept her off court for months and forced her to limit her training thereafter. When a stress fracture of the back forced Boulter to miss another six months in 2019 and the coronavirus pandemic then interrupted her latest comeback the following year, it seemed that good fortune would never be on her side.

By the summer of 2021, nevertheless, Boulter had fought her way back into the world's top 150. Another injury, this time to her left leg, saw her miss the 2022 clay court season, but when it was time to return to grass she was raring to go again. Boulter won three matches in Nottingham and two in Birmingham before claiming the biggest win of her career at Eastbourne when she knocked out Karolina Pliskova, the world No.7, before Petra Kvitova, the eventual champion, beat her 7-5 in the final set in the following round.

When Boulter beat Clara Burel in the first round at The Championships it was her seventh victory over a higher-ranked opponent in less than a month. Now she would face Pliskova again, this time on Centre Court. The last time the 30-year-old Czech had played there had been in the 2021 final, which she lost to Ashleigh Barty, but she had struggled to find her best form since missing the 2022 Australian Open with a hand injury.

Opposite and above: Katie Boulter had waited a long time for her moment in the SW19 spotlight, which came as she defeated last year's runner-up, Karolina Pliskova, on Centre Court

Previous pages: The view from the Hill as a perfect rainbow covers the Grounds

POSITIVE THINKING

—

Be an Environment
Positive Champion.
Share your environment
positive actions
#GreenAtWimbledon

The idea that tennis can save the planet is not quite as far-fetched as it may sound. The All England Club has had an environmental sustainability plan in place since 2020, with the aim of becoming environment positive by 2030.

The most obvious signs of this project are more electric cars in the transport fleet and plenty of recycling points around the Grounds, but in every detail attempts have been made to reuse, recycle and to protect the environment. From the cardboard containers for the strawberries and cream to the reusable drinks cups (they cost £1 which can be reclaimed when the cup is returned); from a new timber-framed building with solar panels that can be dismantled and its component parts repurposed to countertops made from recycled racket strings – it all contributes to the Club's aim to be 'Environment Positive Every Day'.

Having recently recommitted to the UN's Sport for Climate Action Framework, a discussion panel was held on Day Four to raise awareness and encourage behavioural changes in everyone from the fans to the athletes themselves, and everyone else in between. The panel included (*from left to right*): Alexandra Willis (Communications & Marketing Director, AELTC), Melissa Wilson (climate advocate and former international rower), Kate Hughes (Director for International Climate Change, BEIS), Jonathan Overend (BBC), Laura Robson (former British No.1) and Hattie Park (Sustainability Manager, AELTC).

With rain in the air, the match was played under a closed roof, which helped amplify the noise of a crowd who immediately got behind the home player. Boulter won the first two games but Pliskova, soon settling into a good rhythm on her potent serve, took the first set. The second went to a tie-break, which Boulter dominated after winning the first four points. The Briton's booming ground strokes are usually her biggest asset, and in the deciding set she struck the ball with increasing confidence. After breaking serve at 4-4, Boulter served out to complete her 3-6, 7-6(4), 6-4 victory with a winning volley to reach the third round of a Grand Slam event for the first time.

In her on-court interview after the match Boulter was in tears as she dedicated her victory to the memory of her grandmother, who had died two days earlier. She said later that she had spoken on the phone to her grandfather on the eve of her victory over Burel. "He didn't mention anything, but he gave me the inkling that it might be coming," she said. "I didn't know anything until after my first match, when my mum pulled me aside and told me. It's been a tough few days for sure. I've tried to get my emotions out and deal with the situation, try and keep my head on the tennis. I was lucky because my grandpa managed to come down from Leicester, so we could keep him company and keep supporting him at the same time."

The world No.118 said Wimbledon had always been her grandmother's favourite tournament. "That's why it's a special one for me, because she'd watch every single match that was on the TV," Boulter

There was no stopping Liam Broady. Even though he lost a run of 11 games in the middle of the match, he refused to let Diego Schwartzman, the No.12 seed, beat him

said. "She lived just down the road from the tennis club where I started playing. Leicestershire is very close to my heart. I've spent a lot of time on the courts there with my grandparents and my family."

Despite second round defeats for Jack Draper, Alastair Gray and Harriet Dart, who all lost to seeded opponents, The Championships continued to be productive for British players. Heather Watson, returning to Court 18 after her match against Qiang Wang had been halted the previous evening because of bad light, needed only eight minutes to complete a 7-5, 6-4 victory that took her into the third round, while Liam Broady recorded the best result of his career when he beat Diego Schwartzman, the No.12 seed, 6-2, 4-6, 0-6, 7-6(6), 6-1.

Broady had lost to the 29-year-old Argentinian at the same stage 12 months earlier and appeared to be on the ropes when he lost 11 games in a row to lose the third set 6-0 and trail 3-0 in the fourth. However, he had found new resilience over the previous year, during which time he had won his first Challenger title after losing in seven finals and climbed to a career-high position of No.116 in the world. In the fourth set Broady fought back to win a tense tie-break and he went on to dominate the fifth, completing his victory after three hours and 47 minutes. The 28-year-old Briton said afterwards that the defeats of Murray and Raducanu the previous day had actually motivated him. "I wanted to get a little result for the British players myself to give us something to hold on to," he said.

The Fortnight was also developing into a good one for American men, who by the end of the day had secured a quarter of the spots in the last 32, which was the country's most at The Championships since 1995 and the most at any Grand Slam event since 1996. Brandon Nakashima, aged 20, secured the day's most eye-catching victory when he condemned Denis Shapovalov, a semi-finalist 12 months

earlier, to his seventh defeat in eight matches, winning 6-2, 4-6, 6-1, 7-6(6). Jenson Brooksby disposed of Benjamin Bonzi, while Taylor Fritz hit what he described as the best shot of his life in beating Gray in straight sets. Gray, thinking he had saved a set point, fist-pumped in celebration, only for Fritz to hurl himself across the turf and hit a winner into the open court.

Rafael Nadal was still some way below his best in a scratchy 6-4, 6-4, 4-6, 6-3 victory over Ricardas Berankis, but Stefanos Tsitsipas showed notable improvement on his first round performance when he beat Jordan Thompson 6-2, 6-3, 7-5. Meanwhile Roberto Bautista Agut became the third seeded player in the gentlemen's singles draw to withdraw because of Covid.

Nick Kyrgios beat Filip Krajinovic 6-2, 6-3, 6-1 with a ruthless display of controlled aggression and looked a very different man to the temperamental individual who had struggled in the first round. At his post-match media conference Kyrgios complained about what he saw as "disrespect" from the media. "It was just kind of a reminder to put you all back in your place," the Australian said of his 85-minute victory over the No.26 seed. "I just feel like people just don't give me the respect sometimes because of other things that I do. There was just nothing the media possibly could tell me I did wrong today. I just know that you can't possibly ask me anything and stir anything up. And I love it because then you can't write anything. What are you going to say? Nothing today. Dumbfounded all of you."

Iga Swiatek extended her winning run to 37 matches, but the world No.1 was made to struggle by Lesley Pattinama Kerkhove, a 30-year-old Dutchwoman playing in only her fourth Grand Slam event. The world No.138, who owed her place in the draw to Danka Kovinic's withdrawal with injury, capitalised on Swiatek's 31 unforced errors before the top seed scraped home 6-4, 4-6, 6-3.

As is his wont, Rafael Nadal was gradually going through the gears in the early rounds. He dropped a set to Ricardas Berankis but produced some electrifying strokes

FOUR SEASONS IN ONE SET

It rains, it shines; it blows, it thunders – welcome to the British summer. On Day Four we had blue sky, rain clouds and sunshine – sometimes all at the same time (*above and opposite, bottom*). The Wimbledon stalwarts from the Hill, No.1 Court and Centre Court had fortunately come prepared (*below*) and, at the end of the day, a rainbow framed Wimbledon (*opposite, top*). And, of course, there was the ubiquitous Mexican wave as the roof was closed over Centre Court (*right*).

"On grass I feel like everything changes," Swiatek said afterwards. "You have to adjust the movement. I really like how I move on court, especially when I can slide, when I can recover quickly. Here I can't really slide. I have to slow down before hitting the ball, so it's tricky."

Petra Kvitova had no such problems adjusting to her favourite playing surface, though the 2011 and 2014 champion again showed signs of the nerves she has experienced here in recent years when she let slip a 5-1 lead in the second set before beating Ana Bogdan 6-1, 7-6(5). "Every year is a big challenge for me," Kvitova said. "Dealing with the nerves and excitement at the same time is always a bit tough. This year, so far, it's OK. It's not the best, but it's not the worst as well. I'm still hanging in there."

Elena Rybakina beat Bianca Andreescu, the 2019 US Open champion, 6-4, 7-6(5), while Harmony Tan, the conqueror of Serena Williams, knocked out Sara Sorribes Tormo, the No.32 seed. Simona Halep, the 2019 champion, trailed in both sets against Kirsten Flipkens before winning 7-5, 6-4. Coco Gauff had no such problems against Mihaela Buzarnescu, winning 6-2, 6-3 in just 70 minutes and hitting what would prove to be the fastest serve of the Fortnight by a female player at 124mph. The 18-year-old American, who had reached the fourth round in both her previous appearances at The Championships, said it was the first time she had not felt nervous walking on to Centre Court. "I do feel like it's a home court for me," she said. "The majority of the time when I'm playing on that court, I would say the majority of the crowd is with me."

Unnoticed and untroubled, Elena Rybakina was happily signing autographs and helping the fans take selfies on Court 12. Little did she or the autograph hunters know what was going to happen in the coming days

DAILY DIARY DAY 4

There was barely a dry eye on No.2 Court as Kirsten Flipkens (*above*) waved farewell to Wimbledon for the last time. At the age of 36, the former semi-finalist was retiring after her loss to Simona Halep. "When I came here for the first time, Kim Clijsters was actually playing here in the juniors and I was like: "Wow – once in my life I want to play here," she told the crowd afterwards. "Wimbledon was always top of my bucket list. It will always be so special for me and I'm really happy and grateful that I could say goodbye on this court against this champion with a crowd like you guys." The crowd – which included her compatriot Clijsters – responded with a standing ovation and much wiping away of tears. So, what was next for Kirsten? She looked wistful and said: "That's a good question..." before suddenly remembering, "Oh, doubles tomorrow! And then I'm going to Ibiza!"

• Alex de Minaur had just come from a set down to beat Britain's Jack Draper in front of a partisan crowd on No.1 Court. He was a happy man. "Stoked" was the term he used; he was "stoked" to be through to the third round for the second time in his career. Not that he was keen to talk about that in his on-court interview. "Before we talk about my match, can we just talk about Katie Boulter today?" he said. "She had a pretty good win

herself!" Was this some vain attempt to get the crowd to forgive him for beating one of their own? No, this was a very proud Australian pointing out that his girlfriend, Britain's No.4, had caused the shock of the day in taking down last year's finalist.

• Like the first cuckoo of spring, the first official sighting of Dame Mary Berry means that Wimbledon really is in full swing. Dame Mary (*left*) loves Wimbledon and all its traditions, and on Day Four she took her place in the Royal Box. Trying desperately hard to refrain from using the drawerful of bad baking jokes available (all right then, just one: did the lack of rain mean there were no 'soggy bottoms'?), we can reveal that when interviewed by the Wimbledon Radio Channel in the morning, she talked enthusiastically and informatively about strawberries and about cake... but she was keen to point out that the champagne was very, very good. She knows her onions, does Dame Mary.

Serena Williams had done so much in recent years to draw attention to the challenges facing mothers who returned to competition that Tatjana Maria's comeback had gone largely unnoticed. But in fact Williams, whose daughter Olympia was born in 2017, had no doubt been encouraged in her own comeback by the example of Maria, who was a neighbour in Palm Beach Gardens, Florida.

The 34-year-old German, who in her first matches at The Championships for three years had beaten Astra Sharma in the first round before knocking out Sorana Cirstea, the No.26 seed, in the second, had returned not once but twice: having taken a break after giving birth to her first child, Charlotte, at the end of 2013, she took another after having her second, Cecilia, in April 2021.

Having reached a career-high position of No.46 in the world in 2017, she had made the third round of a Grand Slam event only once before, at The Championships 2015, and had fallen at the first hurdle in her last 10 Grand Slam appearances. Now her third round opponent was Maria Sakkari, the No.5 seed and one of the game's most improved players. Sakkari, who had beaten Maria in the first round of the Australian Open in January, dropped serve at 3-4 in the first set, which the German then took by holding to love. Sakkari failed to serve out for the second set at 5-3 and Maria won the last four games to take the match 6-3, 7-5. "To win against Sakkari today is pretty awesome," Maria said afterwards. "I think I played a good match from the beginning to the end."

Maria, who in April had become the first mother-of-two to win a Tour-level title when she triumphed in Bogota, is coached by her husband, Charles Maria. When she continued practising during her first pregnancy he helped her switch to a one-handed backhand. After both births she

returned to competition within four months. "I don't like to practise for a whole year and then come back on the Tour," she said. "I like to play. I need matches to get back in shape."

Tatjana, Charles and their two children travel on tour as a family. Charlotte, who is home-schooled by her mother, enjoys playing tennis and loves life on tour. "She wants to stay super-long everywhere we stay, so that puts extra pressure on me," Maria said. "She tells me: 'Mum, you have to win today because we have to stay.' When we asked her what she thought about us having a third child she said: 'No, no, we can't have another break'!"

If playing in the third round was an unfamiliar experience for Maria, it certainly was not for Elise Mertens, the 26-year-old Belgian having reached the last 32 on her last 18 Grand Slam appearances. Although she has had more success in doubles, Mertens was still seeded No.24 in singles and demonstrated her ability with a 6-4, 7-5 victory over Angelique Kerber, the 2018 champion and No.15 seed. Kerber, who was playing in her 51st consecutive Grand Slam event on a run that dated back to the US Open of 2009, had won more matches on grass (84) than any currently active women other than the Williams sisters, but on this occasion she made too many unforced errors – 28 compared with Mertens' tally of 14. The 34-year-old German led 5-3 in the second set before Mertens seized back the initiative.

Mertens' next opponent would be Ons Jabeur, who was continuing to show why many saw her as a favourite for the title. The 27-year-old Tunisian had dropped a total of just eight games in her first two matches, against Mirjam Bjorklund and Katarzyna Kawa, and was in a hurry again, beating Diane Parry 6-2, 6-3. In three matches Jabeur had spent a total of just three hours and six minutes on court. "I love playing here," the No.3 seed said afterwards. "I want to keep it as short as I can. For now I'm just really enjoying playing on grass."

Lesia Tsurenko, who had matched her best run at The Championships by reaching the third round, was beaten 4-6, 6-3, 3-6 by Germany's Jule Niemeier. The Ukrainian blamed her defeat on "mental overload", saying she had felt nervous all day. "I know that there is a war at home, and I think it

Heather Watson was all smiles after she beat Kaja Juvan from Slovenia to reach the second week of Wimbledon for the first time in her career

just makes me too nervous sometimes," she said. "It's just like some part of me is always so tight. I think it will be a big release when the war will finish, but not before."

At her 43rd attempt Heather Watson finally achieved her goal of reaching the second week of a Grand Slam event when she beat Kaja Juvan 7-6(6), 6-2. Watson, appearing at The Championships for the 12th time, was playing for the fifth day in a row after her first two matches were both spread over two days. After winning an edgy tie-break at the end of the first set, the 30-year-old Briton ran away with the second, though she faltered slightly after taking a 5-0 lead.

Watson has often saved her best performances for The Championships but had fallen in the third round on three previous occasions, most notably in 2015, when she came within two points of beating Serena Williams. "I've been in the third round quite a few times here at

CHAIRMAN'S SPECIAL GUESTS

—

They are some of the most prized seats in the world: the 74 Lloyd Loom wicker chairs in the Royal Box. Every day throughout the Fortnight, the Chairman, Ian Hewitt, invites friends and guests of the Club for lunch, tea and then drinks at the end of play as well as a day of spectacular tennis.

This year, the guest list had a theme that ran across the 14 days: people who work to make society better for all. These guests came from all areas of public service and business. A familiar face to many in Britain during the pandemic, Sir Jonathan Van-Tam, the former Deputy Chief Medical Officer for England, was present on Day 12, while the similarly familiar Sir Patrick Vallance, Chief Scientific Adviser to the UK Government, attended on Day 10.

Dr Dame Jennifer Harries (*above, right*) with Ian Hewitt, Chairman of the All England Club, saw Iga Swiatek open her campaign on Day Two. Dame Jennifer is the Chief Executive of the UK Health Security Agency, and she too played a vital role in the country's response to the pandemic. Also present that day was The Right Honourable Professor Lord Kakkar (*right*), the Professor of Surgery, University College London, who sits on the cross benches in the House of Lords and who in 2020 was a commissioner for the Commission on Race and Ethnic Disparities.

On Sporting Saturday there were also, of course, the usual tributes to sporting and creative prowess, including Hannah Cockroft OBE, British wheelchair racer and multiple Paralympic gold medallist (*above*).

STRONG FAMILY TIES

His brother, Andy, had partnered her sister, Serena, back in 2019. Now it was time for the older siblings to join forces. The rumours had been circulating for days that Jamie Murray and Venus Williams would play together in the mixed doubles after Venus asked for a late wild card. Initially, she had only planned on coming to England to watch Serena at Eastbourne and then in SW19, but then, in her own words, she "saw the grass and got excited". Now she and Jamie were on No.1 Court and beating Michael Venus and Alicja Rosolska. Some families just work well together...

Wimbledon and the Australian Open, so I was just sort of waiting for it to happen," she said afterwards. "I thought I played really well today. As each match has gone by, I've been playing better and better."

Another Briton, Cameron Norrie, also booked his place in the fourth round of a Grand Slam event for the first time. The No.9 seed, who had lost in the third round to Roger Federer 12 months earlier, crushed Steve Johnson 6-4, 6-1, 6-0 on Centre Court in an hour and 50 minutes to become the first British man to reach the last 16 in singles at Wimbledon since Andy Murray in 2017. Johnson, a big-serving American, was in the contest until he was broken in the final game of the opening set but lost 13 of the last 14 games. "It feels really good to do it here at Wimbledon," Norrie said when asked about his achievement in reaching the fourth round. "I definitely enjoyed that match today. I'm really enjoying playing at this level, enjoying the process of it all, and enjoying improving."

At this stage of the Fortnight no player had made bigger strides in recent weeks than Tim van Rijthoven, who had begun the grass court season ranked No.205 in the world, having never won a match at Tour-level. The 25-year-old Dutchman, who had previously lost three years of his career to major injuries, began his grass court campaign with a defeat in the first round of a Challenger at Surbiton but then went on a stunning run on home soil at 's-Hertogenbosch. After beating Taylor Fritz and Felix Auger-Aliassime en route to the final, Van Rijthoven won the title with a straight-sets victory over Daniil Medvedev, the world No.2.

Tim van Rijthoven had never won a match on grass until this year but now he was on a roll – his win over Nikoloz Basilashvili extended his unbeaten run to eight matches

The sorcerer and his apprentice – Novak Djokovic strides out to face fellow Serb Miomir Kecmanovic, who had surged up the rankings since the start of the year

That earned Van Rijthoven a wild card at The Championships, which he quickly justified with some memorable performances. Having accounted for Federico Delbonis and the No.15 seed, Reilly Opelka, in his first two matches, the Dutchman won his eighth match in a row on grass when he beat Nikoloz Basilashvili, the No.22 seed, 6-4, 6-3, 6-4. "From the outside it obviously looks like a fairytale because it came out of nowhere for a lot of people," Van Rijthoven said afterwards. "It's basically a sum-up of a lot of hard work, a lot of belief, and eventually very positive vibes just going into matches and going into practices." His next opponent would be Novak Djokovic, who crushed fellow Serb Miomir Kecmanovic 6-0, 6-3, 6-4.

Jannik Sinner, aged 20, knocked out Andy Murray's conqueror, John Isner, to become the youngest Italian man to reach the fourth round in the Open era. Isner hit 24 aces, but it was Sinner who did not have to defend any break points in the match, his all-round quality proving too hard for the American to break down. The No.10 seed's 6-4, 7-6(4), 6-3 victory set up an intriguing last 16 encounter with 19-year-old Carlos Alcaraz, who overwhelmed Oscar Otte 6-3, 6-1, 6-2. Frances Tiafoe, the No.23 seed, enjoyed a 3-6, 7-6(1), 7-6(3), 6-4 victory over Alexander Bublik, who hit six underarm serves in one game – only two of which found the court.

DAILY DIARY **DAY 5**

Greater love hath no man than one who overshadows his greatest win with his devotion to his football club. So it was that Liam Broady (*above*) celebrated his pulsating, five-set triumph over No.12 seed Diego Schwartzman to reach the third round by putting his fingers in his ears a la Jack Grealish. The Manchester City star did the same thing when he scored his first goal for his new club following his record-breaking £100 million move from Aston Villa. Liam, a mad-keen City fan, explained afterwards that Grealish was his favourite player. And the City man responded in kind by putting out a tweet on Day Five: "What a guy! Can't wait for tomorrow!! You got all our support bro!! Cammmmmm on sannnn!"

• There is more that goes into a Wimbledon title challenge than just practicing and playing, as Novak Djokovic discovered in the first week of The Championships 2022. Apparently, his two children, Stefan and Tara, think that anyone who plays at Wimbledon is a superhero. Well, anyone other than their dad, that is. Like many of the players, Djokovic rents a house close to the All England Club during the Fortnight, and to keep the kids happy he tried to put up a trampoline in the garden for them. At first all was going reasonably well – frame assembled, just the bouncy bit in the middle to fit – but then he came unstuck. He employed the help of his coach, Goran Ivanisevic, but still they could not get the tarpaulin to attach to the springs. As the two men sweated and grimaced and tried to get bit A to fit into slot B, young Stefan piped up: "You can play at Wimbledon but you can't put up a trampoline!" Out of the mouths of babes and innocents...

• John Isner (*left*) made history on No.2 Court as he took on Jannik Sinner. At 6ft 10in, the American has a serve that has struck terror into the hearts of all who have stood before it for the better part of two decades. Against the No.10 seed, he needed just five more aces to break Ivo Karlovic's world record of 13,728 delivered over the course of a career. Needless to say, those five were pinged down in his first two service games. But while Big John went on to serve 24 aces in all, it was his Italian rival who actually aced it as Sinner won in straight sets.

Since his initial breakthrough at Wimbledon in 2014, Nick Kyrgios' worldwide fame – or, depending on your viewpoint, his notoriety – had rarely derived from being able to make a serious challenge for the biggest prizes. The 27-year-old Australian arrived at The Championships having never gone beyond the singles quarter-finals at a Grand Slam event; the last time he had gone that far had been in Melbourne in 2015.

Above: Saturday night fever – temperatures ran high throughout their match but in between the drama Nick Kyrgios and Stefanos Tsitsipas produced some spectacular tennis

Previous pages: By the left, quick, smile! Ball Boys and Girls line up outside Centre Court

While it was true that he had rarely followed a full schedule – and indeed had played only nine events in two years after the outbreak of the coronavirus pandemic – his career-to-date tally of five ATP titles was a meagre return for a player of such outrageous natural talent. He had beaten Novak Djokovic in both their meetings and had registered wins over Roger Federer, Rafael Nadal and Andy Murray.

While Kyrgios can be a wonderful player to watch thanks to his ball-striking ability, ingenuity and unpredictability, he can also be a volcano in danger of erupting at any moment. Rarely afraid to speak his mind, he had had regular run-ins with officials and had even spoken of his dislike for tennis, saying he would rather have been a basketball player.

The one thing you could say with certainty about the world No.40 was that he has great box office appeal, especially among younger fans. His third round encounter with Stefanos Tsitsipas, the dashing world No.5, at prime time on Saturday evening was one of the most eagerly awaited matches of the first week. Tsitsipas had just won his first title on grass in Mallorca, while Kyrgios had already shown both sides of his character in his first two matches. Petulant and distracted as he laboured to beat Paul Jubb, he had played superbly – and behaved impeccably – against Filip Krajinovic.

Which Kyrgios would turn up on No.1 Court? We soon had the answer as the Australian began sounding off after only three games. In the tie-break at the end of a tight first set a line judge reported Kyrgios to Damien Dumusois, the umpire, for bad language. When he was reported for a second time, Dumusois issued a code violation.

Tsitsipas won the tie-break, but when Kyrgios broke to take the second set the 23-year-old Greek thrashed the ball away in frustration. Now it was Tsitsipas' turn to receive a code violation, though Kyrgios complained that he should have been defaulted for hitting a ball into the crowd. Kyrgios demanded to see the supervisor, who backed the umpire. Kyrgios then asked Dumusois to "bring out more supervisors" and said he would not continue playing "until we get to the bottom of this". The match nevertheless resumed, but when Kyrgios hit an underarm serve Tsitsipas lost his cool again, thrashing a wild return, for which he was handed a second code violation and a point penalty.

Tsitsipas' fury was evident, but, amid all the mayhem, some wonderful tennis was played. Kyrgios, barely stopping to draw breath between points, served beautifully and hit some stunning winners, while Tsitsipas' forehand crackled with aggression. Kyrgios took the third set, had a slight dip after the roof was closed at 4-4 in the fourth because of the fading light but then saved two set points before completing his 6-7(2), 6-4, 6-3, 7-6(7) victory after more than three hours.

The sniping continued in the post-match media conferences. Tsitsipas accused Kyrgios of being a bully with "a very evil side" to his character. "He was probably a bully at school himself," Tsitsipas said. "Every single point that I played today, I feel like there was something going on on the other side of the net. I tried not to be distracted by that, because I know it might be intentional, because for sure he can play another way. That's his way of manipulating the opponent and making you feel distracted. There is no other player that does this, that is so upset and frustrated all the time with something. I really hope all us players can come up with something and make this a cleaner version of our sport, have this kind of behaviour not accepted, not allowed, not tolerated."

Four sets, more than three hours and a code violation later, Nick Kyrgios roars with delight as he reaches the fourth round

Kyrgios, who said Tsitsipas had "serious issues", countered: "I'm not sure how I bullied him. He was the one hitting balls at me, he was the one that hit a spectator, he was the one that smacked it out of the stadium." The Australian added: "I've got many friends in the locker room, just to let you know. I'm actually one of the most liked. I'm set. He's not liked. Let's just put that there."

Tsitsipas was subsequently fined $10,000 for unsportsmanlike conduct and Kyrgios $4,000 for swearing, but the debate over their behaviour continued. A leading article in *The Times* said that tennis "does itself a disservice if it allows showmanship to trump sportsmanship, particularly when showmanship starts to look like gamesmanship". Mats Wilander said on Eurosport that he had "never seen anything like it" and added: "I'm not sure I want to see something like that again." Pat Cash told the BBC that Kyrgios had "brought tennis to the lowest level I can see as far as gamesmanship, cheating, manipulation, abuse, aggressive behaviour to umpires, to linesmen."

While Kyrgios and Tsitsipas were feuding there was also acrimony on Centre Court, where Rafael Nadal played his best match of the Fortnight so far to beat Lorenzo Sonego 6-1, 6-2, 6-4. Nadal complained to the Italian for grunting loudly in the middle of a rally, which prompted a lengthy discussion between the two men at the end of the match. Nadal nevertheless admitted afterwards that he had been wrong to call out Sonego during the match and said he had apologised to him in the locker room.

Alex de Minaur beat Britain's Liam Broady 6-3, 6-4, 7-5 to reach the last 16 for the first time, while another Australian, Jason Kubler, beat Jack Sock 6-2, 4-6, 5-7, 7-6 (4), 6-3 after four and a quarter hours in the first third round match between qualifiers at The Championships for 38 years. For 29-year-old Kubler it was a reward for perseverance, the former world junior No.1 having undergone six knee operations in his early twenties.

Iga Swiatek's 37-match winning run, which had seen the 21-year-old Pole win six tournaments in a row, including Roland-Garros, was finally ended when she was beaten 4-6, 2-6 by Alize Cornet. One more victory would have seen Swiatek beat Martina Hingis' winning streak in 1997 and establish the longest unbeaten run since Steffi Graf won 66 matches in a row between 1989 and 1990. Swiatek, who had been taken to a third set by a qualifier in the previous round, again made too many mistakes, which she blamed on tactical confusion. "For sure I didn't have as much belief [on grass] as on other surfaces," the world No.1 said.

Right: An animated Rafael Nadal and Lorenzo Sonego discuss matters of on-court etiquette. Nadal would later apologise, explaining he overreacted

Opposite: Nadal produced his best performance of The Championships so far to beat Sonego – the No.27 seed – in straight sets

CENTRE COURT

THE WIMBLEDON EXPERIENCE

—

No.1 COURT

It is easy to assume that because you have been watching Wimbledon on the television for a lifetime, you will know where you are going when you get there. But even the biggest screen cannot give a true idea of quite how vast and busy the 42 acres of the All England Club are. In order to make your visit as smooth and enjoyable as possible, this year a raft of new ideas were introduced to further enhance the experience.

There was new signage everywhere which made navigation easier – even to the experienced eye one outside court can look alarmingly like another, particularly if you are trying to meet your friend on Court 4. There were new maps around the Grounds, all redesigned to be user-friendly and easy to read as you passed. Just in case, there were also helpful guides on hand to offer directions.

For those who wanted the full details of who was playing whom on which court, the IBM Information Boards were invaluable. And if someone fancied a brief break from the on-court drama, there was plenty to do, from having a go at restringing a racket to having your photograph taken with replicas of the famous trophies.

Then there were the 'Recognition Postcards'. On these, AELTC colleagues could give the name of anyone whom they had observed going out of their way to be helpful to guests. The top four helpers named over the Fortnight were invited to the Champions' Dinner.

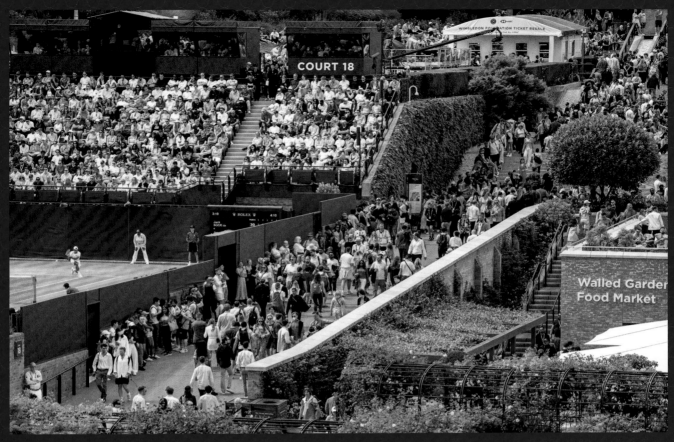

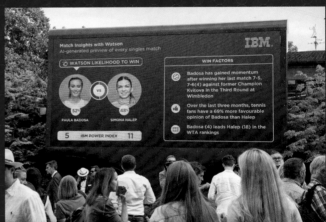

Coco Gauff, another of the title favourites, also went out, beaten 7-6(4), 2-6, 1-6 by Amanda Anisimova in a meeting between two young Americans who can look ahead to many years of rivalry. Gauff, aged 18, had reached the fourth round on both her previous appearances at The Championships but was outhit by 20-year-old Anisimova, who had also beaten her in the 2017 US Open girls' final. "It was a super tough match today, but it was extremely special to get to play on Centre Court for the first time," Anisimova said afterwards. "I was trying to soak in every moment."

Paula Badosa also made a memorable Centre Court debut as the No.4 seed beat Petra Kvitova 7-5, 7-6(4) to reach the fourth round for the second year in a row. Kvitova served for the first set at 5-4, but the two-times champion made too many unforced errors. There were no breaks of serve in the second set, in which Badosa saved all nine break points against her.

"For me one of the biggest challenges is to play Petra on grass," Badosa said afterwards. "Today, being able to play against her it was already a pleasure. You can't imagine how I feel after this win. It's unbelievable. I remember in 2014 I came here to play juniors and one of the first matches I watched was on Centre Court, Petra winning Wimbledon. So you can imagine, for me stepping on Centre Court for the first time playing against a legend like her is really, really special. She's been an inspiration for me."

Simona Halep eased to a 6-4, 6-1 victory over Magdalena Frech, while Harmony Tan continued her remarkable week by beating Katie Boulter 6-1, 6-1 in just 51 minutes. "I think I like grass," the Frenchwoman said after winning three Tour-level matches in a row for the first time in her career. "I really like to play with some slice, volley, everything with my game." Boulter, who had beaten Karolina Pliskova twice during the best grass court season of her career, admitted: "I think I'm just a little bit emotionally drained, if I'm honest. It's been a long few weeks."

Another Briton, Kyle Edmund, made a welcome return to competition in the mixed doubles alongside Olivia Nicholls. The former world No.14 had undergone three knee operations since his last appearance in October 2020 and admitted he had had "a long time to think about my first match back". The Britons were beaten 4-6, 1-6 by Sock and Gauff, but Edmund smiled: "It was definitely good to be out there."

Powerful strokes from the back of the court saw Amanda Anisimova come back from a set down to beat Coco Gauff

DAILY DIARY DAY 6

Alize Cornet (*above*) caused the upset of the day – or possibly the week – by snapping Iga Swiatek's unbeaten run of 37 matches, the longest run recorded this century. But Alize was also making history of her own: this was her 62nd consecutive appearance at a Grand Slam, matching Ai Sugiyama's record set in 2009. And all this after announcing in January that this was probably going to be her last year on tour. "I think that's why I'm playing so good," she said. "It's because I know it's almost the end. I'm giving everything." There was that and the fact that she thought she was like a good wine: "In France, good wine always ages well." She should know...

• One visitor caused an unexpected stir when they arrived at the Grounds with an assistance dog. Getting the dog in was no problem – everyone is welcome in SW19 – it was just when the tennis began that problems started. The dog, well-trained and on best behaviour, was doing its job perfectly. Or it was until it saw a ball being struck. It barked. The ball was returned. The dog barked again. Every time a ball was struck, it barked. Eventually both dog and owner were politely asked to move along.

• She had just won her third round match; she had just beaten last year's Roland-Garros champion, Barbora Krejcikova. But now Ajla Tomljanovic was homeless. Her father, clearly not expecting her to repeat her feats of last summer when she reached the quarter-finals, had only booked their accommodation for one week. "He's like: 'Ajla, hungry rats swim the fastest.' Whatever that means; some old fatherly saying," she said, sounding somewhat unimpressed. "I'm like: 'Well, I'm not a rat and I'm not hungry! I just want my house from the beginning till the end. Or maybe you should just believe in me a little more!'"

• Could the lady in the sparkly jacket please take it off? Dame Anna Wintour (*below*), the editor of American Vogue and possibly the chicest tennis follower in town,

arrived on No.2 Court sporting a gold jacket and looking, as ever, cool and elegant. She had come to watch Richard Gasquet take on Botic van de Zandschulp but no sooner had she sat down than Gasquet hit three consecutive double faults, and four in all, to drop serve. History does not record whether Gasquet is a dedicated follower of fashionistas.

There was a neat symmetry about the introduction of scheduled play on Middle Sunday that Captain Stanley Peach, the architect who had designed Centre Court, would no doubt have appreciated. It felt entirely appropriate that one of the biggest changes to the schedule in the history of The Championships should coincide with the 100th anniversary of the opening of the world's most iconic tennis stadium.

The timing was a reflection once again of the All England Club's commitment to both tradition and innovation. The day began with a ceremony to mark a century of competition in Captain Peach's creation before proceeding with the first programme of scheduled play on Middle Sunday since the first staging of The Championships in 1877.

The ceremony, hosted by Sue Barker and John McEnroe, was an occasion to remember for all who were present. Its highlight was a parade of past singles champions, who were each given a rapturous welcome by the crowd as they walked into the stadium where they had enjoyed the finest moments of their sporting lives. It seems only right to list every one of them (in order of their appearance): Angela Mortimer, Ann Jones, Stan Smith, Jan Kodes, Pat Cash, Conchita Martinez, Martina Hingis, Goran Ivanisevic, Lleyton Hewitt, Marion Bartoli, Angelique Kerber, Simona Halep, Stefan Edberg, Rafael Nadal, Petra Kvitova, Andy Murray, Margaret Court, John Newcombe, Chris Evert, John McEnroe, Rod Laver, Bjorn Borg, Venus Williams, Billie Jean King, Novak Djokovic and Roger Federer. Martina Navratilova had been due to take part but had gone down with Covid that morning, while others missing had not been able to make the trip for a variety of reasons.

The crowd, who were delighted to hear Federer say he hoped to play at The Championships "one more time", enjoyed video montages of memorable moments in Wimbledon history as well as two musical treats. Sir Cliff Richard emerged in the stands, microphone in hand, to reprise his 1996 rain-delay singalong of *Summer Holiday,* with Pam Shriver among those providing backing vocals just as she

had 26 years earlier, before Freya Ridings, sitting behind a white piano, sang *Lost Without You*. McEnroe then invited the crowd to pay tribute to Barker, his broadcasting colleague, who was presenting at The Championships for the BBC for the last time before retiring. Barker was in tears after receiving a standing ovation. "That really does mean the world to me," she said.

How do you follow an occasion like that? Most of the Centre Court crowd would have been hoping that Heather Watson could prolong the celebrations in the opening match on Centre Court, but the 30-year-old Briton was overpowered by Jule Niemeier, a big-hitting German who had knocked out Anett Kontaveit, the No.2 seed, in the second round. Niemeier, who had made her Grand Slam debut at Roland-Garros only the previous month, won their fourth round encounter 6-2, 6-4 in just an hour and 17 minutes. "I felt like the match was kind of flat because of the style of play," Watson said afterwards. "The points were just so quick."

One home player, nevertheless, did make it through to the quarter-finals as Cameron Norrie beat Tommy Paul 6-4, 7-5, 6-4 on No.1 Court. The No.9 seed, who dropped his serve just once in the match, became only the fifth British man in the Open era to reach the last eight, after

Above: Sir Cliff Richard sings Summer Holiday, just as he did during a Centre Court rain delay in 1996

Left: Sue Barker and John McEnroe hosted the celebration – with McEnroe opening with "Hello Wimbledon!"

Below: Freya Ridings sings Lost Without You to bring the celebration to a close

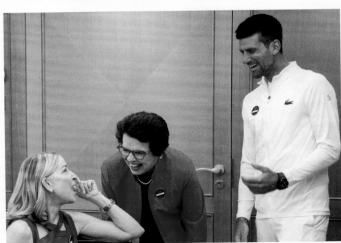

THE LEGENDS LOUNGE

A happy reunion (*this page, clockwise from above*): Roger Federer shakes hands with Rod Laver; Ann Jones and Angela Mortimer share a memory; Ian Hewitt, Chairman of the AELTC, and Martina Hingis chat animatedly; Andy Murray taking it in before he is introduced; Angelique Kerber and Simona Halep enjoy the build-up. *Opposite page, clockwise from top:* Venus Williams enjoys a selfie with Bjorn Borg; Stan Smith makes his point to Jan Kodes, Rod Laver and Bjorn Borg; Andy Murray, Petra Kvitova and Rafael Nadal in discussion; Novak Djokovic, Billie Jean King and Chris Evert share a joke; Rafael Nadal and Roger Federer are all smiles.

PARADE OF CHAMPIONS

Some of the greatest champions to have graced Centre Court came to celebrate its centenary – a historic gathering for a historic stadium. Centre Court had been their stage in the past and now it cheered them to the retractable rafters. *Below (from left to right)*: Angela Mortimer, Rafael Nadal, Stan Smith, Petra Kvitova, Ann Jones, Andy Murray, Jan Kodes, Margaret Court, Pat Cash, John Newcombe, Conchita Martinez, Chris Evert, Goran Ivanisevic, Martina Hingis, Lleyton Hewitt, Bjorn Borg, Rod Laver, Venus Williams, Marion Bartoli, Billie Jean King, Angelique Kerber, Novak Djokovic, Simona Halep, John McEnroe, Stefan Edberg and Roger Federer take the crowd's acclaim; *Left:* Chris Evert waves to the crowd; *Right (clockwise from top left)*: Angela Mortimer and Stan Smith soak up the atmosphere; Novak Djokovic and Roger Federer in conversation; Rod Laver waves as Venus Williams takes in the scene.

Roger Taylor, Tim Henman, Greg Rusedski and Andy Murray. Norrie embraced the idea of being the last home player in singles on whom the crowd could pin their hopes. "I think it's even more reason for everyone to get behind me," he said. "The atmosphere was great today and definitely helped me get over the line. Especially in the last game, I was pretty nervous. I was serving for my first quarter-final of a Slam. I wanted to get it done there. They definitely helped me a lot."

On a day which had begun by looking back on the past, Jannik Sinner and Carlos Alcaraz provided a vision of the future in the second match on Centre Court. Sinner, aged 20, and Alcaraz, aged 19, were the youngest players left in the gentlemen's singles. Indeed, it was the youngest singles match-up here in the fourth round or later in terms of the players' combined age since 17-year-old Boris Becker met 21-year-old Henri Leconte in the quarter-finals in 1985.

In an era mostly dominated by older players, the Italian and the Spaniard had already broken into the world's top 10. Alcaraz had blazed a remarkable trail in the previous 14 months, climbing from No.120 in the world rankings to No.7. Both men, nevertheless, had something to prove on grass, having arrived at The Championships with just one Tour-level victory on the surface between them. Sinner set the pace in a high-energy contest full of spectacular shot-making and athleticism. From 1-1 in the opening set Sinner won seven games in a row and soon had two sets in the bag. Alcaraz saved two match points in a third set tie-break and three more when serving at 2-5 in the fourth set before Sinner secured his 6-1, 6-4, 6-7(8), 6-3 victory.

Sinner hopes the two men will go on to develop a great rivalry. "I think what we showed today, it's a great level of tennis, great attitude from both of us," he said. "I think it's also just great for tennis to have some new names, new players." Alcaraz agreed, saying he hoped the two men would "fight together for the best tournaments in the world and the best moments".

Sheer delight from Cameron Norrie – a straight sets win over his friend Tommy Paul had put him through to his first Grand Slam quarter-final

It might have been a sign of a changing landscape in men's tennis that only three 30-somethings – Nadal, Djokovic and David Goffin – had made it to the last 16. Goffin, aged 31, outlasted Frances Tiafoe, aged 24, in a marathon spread across more than four and a half hours on No.2 Court, beating the No.23 seed 7-6(3), 5-7, 5-7, 6-4, 7-5. Meanwhile Djokovic was pushed hard on Centre Court by the 25-year-old Dutch wild card, Tim van Rijthoven, who had enjoyed a memorable Wimbledon debut. Djokovic won 6-2, 4-6, 6-1, 6-2.

Having started the day by taking part in the ceremony to celebrate Centre Court's 100th anniversary, Djokovic finished it playing under the stadium's closed roof, his match ending at 10.40pm. The defending champion said afterwards that he would prefer each day's programme to start earlier, claiming that The Championships had become "really an indoor tournament in most of the cases when you're scheduled last on Centre or No.1 Court".

Sally Bolton, the All England Club's Chief Executive, defended the scheduling and start times (1pm on No.1 Court and 1.30pm on Centre Court for the first 12 days). "When we look at the scheduling we think as much as we can about what the day is going to look like, and the experience for our guests, but ultimately once the players walk on to court we don't have any control over how long matches run for," she said. "We have seen some matches go late this year and we think about that in the scheduling process, but we are certainly not moving to night sessions and we are not seeking to have players playing late as a matter of routine."

Jelena Ostapenko showed that petulance was not the preserve of male players when she reacted angrily to her 7-5, 5-7, 5-7 defeat by Tatjana Maria, who beat a seeded opponent for the third round in a row. Ostapenko, who had failed to convert two match points in the second set, hurled a water bottle at her chair at the end before storming off the court to boos from the crowd. Having taken the first

Carlos Alcaraz – aged 19 – could not find a way to stop Jannik Sinner – aged 20 – in the battle of the young guns

1922

THAT WAS THEN...

—

There is, quite simply, no place like it. The Boston Ivy-clad walls, the perfect silence before a serve is struck, the dark green everywhere that ensures that neither player nor spectator ever loses sight of the ball, and the explosion of noise when a winner lands. Centre Court is the centre of tennis.

However, when it was first built 100 years ago, there was much sucking of teeth. The naysayers thought it was too big ("It will never be full," they said...) and too ugly (thousands of tons of concrete – on what used to be farmland, to boot...) but the Club pressed on. The Championships was growing in popularity and the old Worple Road ground was too small; it was time to move to Church Road and expand.

Employing the skills of Captain Stanley Peach, an architect better known for building power stations, was a bold move but the Club had a vision for the future.

Building started in the autumn of 1921, and on 26 June the following year Leslie Godfree *(above, left)* won the first point of The Championships 1922 – and pocketed the ball as a memento. Gerald Patterson and Suzanne Lenglen *(left)* won the singles titles, and it seems fair to suggest that they would not recognise the action that graces Centre Court today: supreme athletes with high-tech rackets playing under a roof as the rain thunders down outside – it is a world away from 1922. And yet it feels the same. Typically Wimbledon.

2022

...THIS IS NOW

—

set, the No.12 seed had gone 4-1 up in the second before Maria launched her comeback. In a match of rapidly changing fortunes Maria failed to serve out for victory at 5-4 in the deciding set but did not make the same mistake two games later.

Ostapenko was still seething when she came into her post-match press conference. "I thought it was my match to win and she just got so lucky in some moments," the 25-year-old Latvian said. "She didn't really do anything today. She was just waiting for my mistakes." Maria, who had most of the crowd on her side, said that being a mother of two had given her a different sense of perspective. "I do everything out there to live my dreams, but I also know there are more important things outside," she said. "I know my family and my two kids are the most important for me."

Ons Jabeur, the No.3 seed, was given her first serious test of the Fortnight by Elise Mertens but won 7-6(9), 6-4. Jabeur saved five set points in the tie-break at the end of the first set before going on to take her record in the grass court season to nine wins out of nine following her title triumph in Berlin. "I love playing on grass," she said. "I love the connection between nature and me, so hopefully it will continue this way for me."

Venus Williams and Jamie Murray went out of the mixed doubles, losing 6-3, 4-6, 6-7 (16) to Britain's Jonny O'Mara and Alicia Barnett in a second round match that lasted two hours and 12 minutes. Given that Williams had turned 42 the previous month, it seemed a reasonable assumption that this might be the last time we would see a Williams sister on court at The Championships. But we had said that before, hadn't we?

Jule Niemeier was too strong for Heather Watson as they vied for a place in the quarter-finals. Watson described the German's play as "flawless"

DAILY DIARY DAY 7

They came, the champions of past and present, to celebrate 100 years of Centre Court. The plans had been made; the stage had been set. But before anyone placed foot in the famous old arena, Rufus the Hawk (only his closest friends are allowed to call him just 'Rufus') had done his stuff. A Harris hawk of some renown (he has his own Twitter account), he was celebrating 15 years of pigeon 'relocation' duties at Wimbledon. And on this Middle Sunday, of all Middle Sundays, his role was vital. The pigeons always liked the old Centre Court but the retractable roof structure fitted in 2009 now provides perfect roosting conditions for them. But not if Rufus the Hawk has anything to do with it. Sure enough, after his 6am fly past, there was not a Columbidae anywhere to be seen. Roger Federer's immaculate navy blue suit was safe.

• Tommy Paul had prepared well. He had made it into the fourth round by dint of taking down three successive left-handers (Fernando Verdasco, Adrian Mannarino and Jiri Vesely). That took his record against the southpaws to played 19, won 14. Why this ability to deal with the left-handers' game? There are technical reasons involving his impressive backhand (all of which are far too complicated for our brains to process) but practising with Rafael Nadal, one of the greatest lefties of all time, can only have helped. They were hitting together before The Championships began. However, when faced with a fourth leftie – his good friend Cameron Norrie – he was 'left' standing. Cameron won in straight sets.

• A new day, a new tradition. Middle Sunday – once a day of rest – was, for the first time, part of the scheduled programme of play. To mark the moment Wimbledon invited refugees from Ukraine, Afghanistan and Syria who have now settled in the boroughs of Merton and Wandsworth to come and enjoy the tennis. The Ukranian contingent were greeted by Ukraine's Billie Jean King Cup captain Olga Savchuk. Ian Hewitt, Chairman of the All England Club, commented: "I'm delighted that refugees hosted across Merton and Wandsworth will be joining us for play on Middle Sunday at Wimbledon, which we hope will have a very special atmosphere in its first year as part of the tournament schedule. I'm also delighted that, in partnership with the LTA, we have been able to commit an additional £250,000 towards the humanitarian response in Ukraine."

Winning Wimbledon

inning Wimbledon for the first time is a huge moment in the life of any player, but when Simona Halep triumphed at The Championships 2019 you sensed that the achievement had been particularly special. In the evening after her stunning final victory over Serena Williams, Halep wore her new All England Club member's badge with evident pride. Even before The Championships had begun she had been telling people that her main goal was to earn that badge: now she could look forward to returning to Wimbledon as a Club member.

As it turned out, it would be three years before Halep returned. In 2020 The Championships was cancelled because of the pandemic and in 2021 a calf injury kept the former world No.1 on the sidelines. That denied her the chance to open the Centre Court programme on the second day as defending champion, an honour she had been looking forward to ever since her title triumph.

Come The Championships 2022, the 30-year-old Romanian had to wait until the second Monday to play again in the stadium which had been the scene of her finest hour. Having played her first three matches on No.1 Court and No.2 Court, she clearly relished the chance to perform again on her favourite stage. Her opponent, Paula Badosa, the No.4 seed, won the first game, but was then swept aside. Winning the next six games, Halep took the opening set in just 22 minutes, dropping only three points on her serve in the process. In the second set Badosa hung on grimly until Halep broke in the sixth game and went on to complete her 6-1, 6-2 victory in just an hour.

Halep, who had been wearing her member's badge again at the previous day's centenary celebrations, made no secret of her delight. "It's always a pleasure to be back on Centre Court," she said afterwards. "It was the place that I wanted to be today."

Over the previous 15 months there had been times when Halep had considered retiring as she dropped out of the world's top 10 for the first time since 2014 and struggled to recover from the calf injury that kept her out of Roland-Garros and the Olympics in 2021 as well as The Championships. However, recruiting Patrick Mouratoglou, Serena Williams' former coach, was an indication of her determination to fight her way back to the top.

"It means a lot that I'm back in the quarter-finals after I struggled so much with injuries and self-confidence," Halep said after her victory over Badosa. "I worked really hard in the past two or three months. I'm really happy with all that I've done. That's why I'm starting to play better and better. I've got the confidence."

If Halep had been flying under the radar until this point, so too had Elena Rybakina, who had played her first three matches on Courts 11, 12 and 18. The No.17 seed had won her first three matches without dropping a set and now found herself on No.1 Court, where she faced Petra Martic. Another impressive victory, again built on big ground strokes and bold serves, saw 23-year-old Rybakina win 7-5, 6-3 to reach the quarter-finals in only her second appearance at The Championships, having made the fourth round on her debut one year earlier.

Rybakina, who was born and grew up in Russia but changed her allegiance to Kazakhstan when she was 19, had been more interested in ice skating and gymnastics as a child, but tennis became a more attractive sport as she grew taller. "I know that I have this gift," she said. "I'm tall and I play really fast. It's effortless, I would say. It's not something I'm working on in the gym." Asked to describe the way she played, Rybakina responded with a smile and just three words. "Very aggressive tennis."

Two Frenchwomen who had made big headlines earlier in the Fortnight failed to make the last eight. Alize Cornet, who had knocked out Iga Swiatek, lost for the second year in a row to Ajla Tomljanovic,

Another dominant display from Elena Rybakina – who was yet to drop a set at The Championships 2022 – saw her sweep past Petra Martic and into the last eight

who won 4-6, 6-4, 6-3 in a match that featured 16 breaks of serve. Harmony Tan, who had beaten Serena Williams, lost 2-6, 3-6 to Amanda Anisimova, who went through to a Grand Slam quarter-final for the first time since her big breakthrough at Roland-Garros in 2019, when she made the semi-finals.

Anisimova had been finding her feet again after two difficult years following the death of her father, who was also her coach. Having dropped out of the world's top 80 in 2021, the 20-year-old American was now back to No.25. "When I was 17 I didn't really appreciate getting to the semi-finals as much as I probably should have done," she said. "I think it only soaked in a year later, understanding what that was, how much it actually meant to me. Having over a year of not very good results really affects you. When you have losses every week in early rounds, it's very hard to find motivation, but I just kept going. It just took longer than I thought it would. That's why it means so much to me now to have a great year."

Nobody in tennis was having a better year than Rafael Nadal, who kept alive his chances of achieving a pure calendar-year Grand Slam by beating the No.21 seed, Botic van de Zandschulp, 6-4, 6-2, 7-6(6) with his best performance of the Fortnight so far. Van de Zandschulp, who with Tim van Rijthoven and Tallon Griekspoor was spearheading a Dutch revival, had climbed 114 places in the world rankings in the previous 12 months, but once Nadal had broken serve to take the opening set the result rarely looked in doubt. The 36-year-old Spaniard faltered only at the end of the third set when he let slip a 5-2 lead.

It was 12 years since Nadal had won the second of his two Wimbledon titles, but after what he had achieved in the first six months of 2022 he was being viewed as a very serious contender. In January, having just returned after a six-month break following surgery on a chronic condition in his left foot, he had won the Australian Open, coming back from two sets down to beat Daniil Medvedev in an epic final. A rib stress fracture suffered in losing the final in Indian Wells then ended Nadal's run of 20 successive victories since the start of the year. His recovery delayed his entry into the clay court season, but he still went on to triumph at Roland-Garros for the 14th time.

Following his victory over Casper Ruud in France, Nadal revealed that continuing problems with his left foot had been so bad that he had been forced to play with painkilling injections. After Paris he

Amanda Anisimova brought an abrupt end to Harmony Tan's remarkable run at SW19, taking just 74 minutes to secure a 6–2, 6–3 victory

SAYING IT WITH INK

Nick Kyrgios wears his heart on his sleeve in more ways than one – his right arm is covered in a full tattoo sleeve inspired by his love of basketball, while his left arm is decorated with aphorisms and inspirational symbols. His latest inking is the quote "Give a man a mask and he will become his true self" on his left leg. He's not the only person at SW19 with a fondness for ink – Heath Davidson has a double sleeve look (*right*); Tereza Martincova has just the one (*above right*); Thanasi Kokkinakis has butterflies flying up his left thigh (*far right*); while Kristyna Pliskova has a statement 'Yin and Yang' symbol (*opposite, bottom right*).

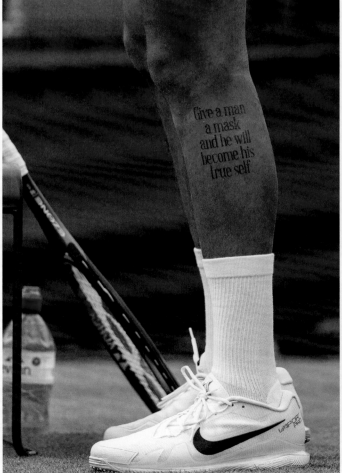

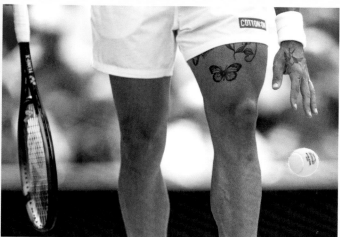
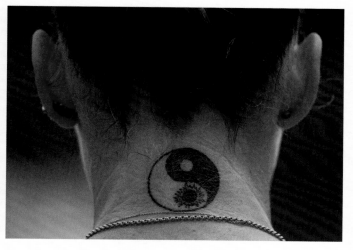

underwent radiofrequency ablation treatment, which applies heat to the nerve to dull pain, and it was only in the week before The Championships that he was able to confirm his participation. "I made a big effort to be here," Nadal said. "It takes a lot of mental and physical effort to try to play this tournament after the things that I went through in the last couple of months."

Nadal's next opponent would be the No.11 seed, Taylor Fritz, who beat Jason Kubler 6-3, 6-1, 6-4 to reach his first Grand Slam quarter-final, thereby emulating his mother, Kathy May, who had made the last eight at both Roland-Garros and the US Open in the 1970s. The highest ranked of a new wave of young Americans, 24-year-old Fritz had won his first Masters 1000 title in March when he beat an ailing Nadal in the Indian Wells final and had won Eastbourne for a second time in the build-up to The Championships.

After his ill-tempered meeting with Stefanos Tsitsipas, Nick Kyrgios was back on his best behaviour against Brandon Nakashima, a 20-year-old American playing in the fourth round of a Grand Slam event for the first time. Kyrgios, who was nursing a sore shoulder, focused on what he described as "an absolute battle" to win 4-6, 6-4, 7-6(2), 3-6, 6-2. The win earned a quarter-final meeting with Cristian Garin, who came back from two sets and 3-0 down, saving two match points along the way, to beat Alex de Minaur 2-6, 5-7, 7-6(3), 6-4, 7-6(6) after four and a half hours.

Kyrgios laughed off the criticism of his behaviour against Tsitsipas. "I don't care," he said. "I just smile. It's so funny. I joke around with my team about it so much. It's hilarious. I almost just wake up and read things and I just laugh. And I never forget things, like the people say, whether it was three, four years ago, things that just stick with me. I have a massive chip on my shoulder. I sit here now in the quarter-finals of Wimbledon again and I just know there's so many people that are so upset."

In the gentlemen's doubles it was not a good day for Britain's Skupski brothers. Neal Skupski and Wesley Koolhof, the No.3 seeds, lost in five sets to Matthew Ebden and Max Purcell, while Ken Skupski and Jonny O'Mara were beaten by Kevin Krawietz and Andreas Mies. For Ken, retiring at the age of 39, it was the final match of a career that had seen him play at The Championships on 14 occasions.

Previous pages: A diving Taylor Fritz was about to land in the quarter-finals as he flew past Jason Kubler in three sets

Below: Jamie Murray and Bruno Soares came unstuck in four sets against John Peers and Filip Polasek in the third round of the gentlemen's doubles

DAILY DIARY DAY 8

It is the greatest tennis show on earth, and on the second Monday some of the most celebrated stars of stage and screen had come to watch. In the Royal Box, Sir Ian McKellen (*above*), Sir Mark Rylance and Sir David Suchet came to see Nick Kyrgios (no overacting this time; just a dogged five-set win), Simona Halep (immaculate performance; only three games dropped) and Rafael Nadal (method acting at its finest, especially the routine with the water bottles; straight sets win) remember their lines and not bump into the furniture on their way to the quarter-finals.

• There are those who like to dress for the occasion when they come to Wimbledon. Some opt for the formal summer attire (Panama hat, linen blazer) and there are some who truly get into the spirit of the event, like the lady from Japan we spotted a few minutes after the gates had opened. She was dressed from head to toe in Wimbledon tennis kit, from her Wimbledon sun visor down to her Wimbledon socks, all newly purchased from the Wimbledon Shop. And she had kept the Wimbledon bag to carry with her the clothes she had worn on her way to the All England Club. But the prize must go to the spectator who arrived dressed as the world's largest tennis ball. If sitting down in that garb must have been difficult, imagine what it must have been like when they tried to avail themselves of the facilities...

• The Championships may be that most British of events, but it usually coincides with the Fourth of July. Not only is that Independence Day but it is also ESPN and Tennis Channel pundit Pam Shriver's birthday – so on the day when most of America is celebrating independence from Britain, Pam can double down. On this particularly special day for their country, several Americans made their presence felt in SW19, with wins for Taylor Fritz (who beat Jason Kubler), Amanda Anisimova (who felled Harmony Tan for the loss of only five games) and for the mixed doubles pair of Coco Gauff and Jack Sock (*below*). Gauff and Sock had both lost in singles on Day Six, but as doubles combo they headed for the quarter-finals on their nation's great holiday with a perfectly timed win over the British pairing of Kyle Edmund and Olivia Nicholls.

- DAY 9 -

TUESDAY 5 JULY

G iven Andy Murray's continuing efforts to recapture former glories and the huge interest in Emma Raducanu following her extraordinary triumph at the US Open, it was perhaps no surprise that the achievements of another Briton, Cameron Norrie, had perhaps not been getting the attention they deserved. In winning his first Masters 1000 title at Indian Wells in October 2021, Norrie had become the men's British No.1. Adding titles at Delray Beach and Lyon in 2022, he had entered the world's top 10.

Now, for the second year in a row, he was the last Briton standing in the gentlemen's singles at The Championships, having reached the second week of a Grand Slam event for the first time. A quarter-final meeting with David Goffin offered an excellent chance of further progress. Goffin, a former world No.7, had recently dropped out of the top 70 for the first time in eight years following some injury issues, though the 31-year-old Belgian had matched his previous best Grand Slam efforts by reaching the last eight here.

The crowd on No.1 Court, which included the Duke and Duchess of Cambridge, who had left their seats in the Royal Box on Centre Court, were treated to an enthralling contest featuring regular momentum shifts. In the early stages in particular Norrie struggled to find the fluency he had shown in beating Steve Johnson and Tommy Paul in straight sets in his two previous matches, but the

26-year-old Briton showed all his battling qualities to regroup after losing two of the first three sets. Breaking Goffin's serve in the eighth game of the fourth set and the 11th game of the decider, he won 3-6, 7-5, 2-6, 6-3, 7-5 after almost three and a half hours to become only the fourth British man in the Open era (after Roger Taylor, Tim Henman and Andy Murray) to reach the Wimbledon singles semi-finals.

Norrie's parents, David and Helen, who are from Glasgow and Cardiff respectively but have lived in New Zealand for more than 20 years, were also in the crowd, along with the No.9 seed's sister and girlfriend. During the pandemic Norrie's parents had been unable to travel, even to watch their son play Roger Federer on Centre Court at The Championships 2021, and the emotion of finally being able to share his joy with them clearly got to the left-hander in his post-match interview on court.

"All the hard work and the sacrifices and everything all hit me at once," he said later. "Especially the situation here at Wimbledon in front of my family, my friends, and obviously a lot of people following that match. I got emotional there. It was just a crazy day and crazy match to get through, especially with the way that it started." Norrie was not the only one to become emotional. "I think every match that I've won this week my mum has cried," he said.

Norrie's years of hard work had begun in New Zealand, his family having moved there from Johannesburg – where he was born – when he was three. He moved to London for the sake of his burgeoning tennis career at the age of 16 and then accepted a scholarship to Texas Christian University (TCU), where he quickly became one of the best players in college tennis in the United States. However, it was only when he had to miss a Challenger tournament in his second year at university after being injured when crashing his moped after a night out that he appreciated the need to be more professional. Facundo Lugones, who was a coach at TCU, has worked with Norrie ever since he started playing on the Tour.

It had been a long road back for David Goffin following a serious knee injury last year, but Cameron Norrie proved to be a step too far for the Belgian

Above: The Duke and Duchess of Cambridge, accompanied by Tim Henman, found time to take in Cameron Norrie's comeback to beat David Goffin, which ended with the British player receiving a standing ovation

Overleaf right: Jannik Sinner had been in charge for two sets until Novak Djokovic moved his game up several gears and left the Italian trailing in his wake

Norrie's flat two-handed backhand is one of his biggest weapons, along with his strength and stamina. They were qualities that he would no doubt need for his next test against Novak Djokovic, who demonstrated his own resilience by coming back from two sets down to beat Jannik Sinner 5-7, 2-6, 6-3, 6-2, 6-2. Sinner, who had never won a match on grass until he arrived at The Championships, made an edgy start, losing the first three games, but once the 20-year-old Italian had conquered his nerves he started playing with all the verve and skill that have made him one of the game's outstanding prospects.

At the end of the second set, however, Djokovic took a bathroom break. "I had a little pep talk with myself in the mirror," the defending champion explained later. "After that, I kind of played a new match. From the start of the third, I played three really very solid, very high-quality tennis sets. From the very beginning of the third when I broke his serve early I felt that I found my rhythm and tempo." In the fifth set Djokovic hit one of the shots of The Championships. Pushed out wide to his backhand, the Serb almost did the splits to reach the ball before somehow driving a winning cross-court passing shot. Afterwards he lay stomach down spread-eagled on the turf, clearly enjoying the moment.

Ons Jabeur, the No.3 seed in the ladies' singles, had not dropped a set in her first four matches but ran into stiff opposition when she faced Marie Bouzkova, a 23-year-old Czech who had never previously gone beyond the second round of a Grand Slam tournament. The world No.66, who had already taken out two seeds in Danielle Collins and Alison Riske-Amritraj, broke serve twice to take the opening set before Jabeur turned the match around. The 27-year-old Tunisian's trademark is the delightful variety of her game as she hits drop shots and wicked spins and slices that can confound the very best, but on this occasion she decided that a more aggressive approach was needed. It worked, as Jabeur won 3-6, 6-1, 6-1 to add to her collection of history-making achievements.

ROYALLY ENTERTAINED

On their first visit to The Championships this year, their Royal Highnesses the Duke and Duchess of Cambridge focused all their attention on the tennis. The Duchess, Patron of the Club and a keen tennis fan, was seen discussing the finer points of the matches with Ian Hewitt, Chairman of the Club (*left*), while also clearly enjoying the Duke's enthusiasm (*below*) as Djokovic completed his thrilling comeback against Jannik Sinner.

TAKING IT TO ANOTHER LEVEL

—

"Insane" is how Cameron Norrie's coach describes the British No.1's fitness. Facundo Lugones has known the 26-year-old since their days together at Texas Christian University and he knows what his charge is capable of. But, even he is amazed by the numbers on the data sheets after a training session.

"He does some really intense conditioning sessions on the court where he stays in that red zone where the heartbeat [up to 200 beats per minute] is just insane," Lugones said. "A normal person can't even do a minute and a half on that. He can play tennis for eight, nine minutes on that." Add to that a lung capacity similar to that of a deep-sea diver and Norrie can run until almost everyone else drops.

Born in South Africa with a Scottish father and a Welsh mother, the family moved to New Zealand when he was a baby. From there he headed to Texas and played college tennis before finally settling in London. When the first lockdown loomed in 2020, Norrie went back to New Zealand and worked even harder on his fitness. Running up and down the hills of Auckland, he got his 10k time down to a personal best of 36 minutes and 45 seconds.

With that level of fitness as his base, he started running up the rankings ladder – from No.74 at the start of last year to No.12 as he cycled into work for the first day of The Championships.

Already the first Arab woman to reach a Grand Slam quarter-final and the first to win a WTA title, Jabeur became only the fourth African woman in the Open era to reach a Grand Slam semi-final (after Annette du Plooy, Yvonne Vermaak and Amanda Coezter) and the first from outside South Africa. In 2011 she had become the first North African woman to win a junior Grand Slam title (at Roland-Garros) and in the spring of 2022 she was the first African to win a WTA 1000 title (in Madrid).

The only Tunisian woman ranked in the world's top 700, Jabeur said that she had been in contact with Hicham Arazi, a former top 25 player from Morocco. "He told me: 'Arabs always lose in the quarter-finals and we are sick of it. Please break this.' I was like: 'I'll try, my friend.' We were just texting and he was really happy. He was like: 'Thank you for finally making the semi-finals. Now you can really go and get the title.'"

Jabeur is one of many who have been helped by support from the Grand Slam Player Development Programme, which was set up by the Grand Slams in 1986 to give more opportunities to players from developing regions. "It's one of the reasons why I'm here today, why I'm winning matches," said Jabeur, who first received support from the programme as a member of a 14-and-under touring team to Europe in 2008.

KIDS ON TOUR

The next generation is already here. Stefan Djokovic is obviously following in his father's footsteps on the practice court (*opposite*). Stefan is only seven but already tries to intimidate his dad (so his dad says...) by copying Rafael Nadal's distinctive forehand (*left*). Tatjana Maria (*above*) began every day during The Championships with a hit with her daughter, Charlotte. Nick Kyrgios (*below*) welcomed the newest wave of talent, congratulating Naomi Broady on the news that she is expecting twins (hence the two Wimbledon babygrows) while Marion Bartoli (*below, left*) took her daughter, Kamilya, on court with her during her Invitation Doubles match.

An emotional embrace between compatriots Tatjana Maria and Jule Niemeier following Maria's hard-fought victory

Since breaking into the world's top 30 for the first time in 2021, Jabeur had gone from strength to strength. This victory, in her ninth quarter-final of an outstanding year, took her tally of match wins in the last two seasons to 83, which was more than any other player on the WTA Tour. It was also her 10th win in a row on grass following her triumph in Berlin in her only warm-up tournament on the surface.

In the semi-finals Jabeur would face another newcomer to this stage of a Grand Slam competition, her good friend Tatjana Maria, who extended the best run of her career by beating her fellow German, Jule Niemeier, 4-6, 6-2, 7-5 on No.1 Court. Niemeier, through to the quarter-finals on her Championships debut at the age of 22, edged a tense first set in which both players looked nervous, but eventually paid the price for failing to find a good rhythm on her serve, which had been one of her most important assets in her earlier matches. Niemeier, who made 54 unforced errors in the match to Maria's 37, hit 11 double faults and only three aces.

At 34 Maria was the oldest first-time women's Grand Slam singles semi-finalist in the Open era. She had begun the day as she had every other, by practising at 8.30am with the older of her two daughters, eight-year-old Charlotte, on the All England Club's indoor courts. "Outside of the court, nothing changes for me," Maria said. "I'm in a Wimbledon semi-final. It's crazy, but I'm still a mum. After this I will see my kids and I will do the same thing I do every single day. I try to keep everything as normal as possible, because what makes me proudest is being a mum."

DAILY DIARY DAY 9

It was the day to welcome back the Invitation Doubles, hugely popular events that had not been held since 2019. The stars of the previous generations were back on court in the ladies' and gentlemen's events – as they had been three years ago – but this time there was also mixed doubles, And in this event the pairings were arranged by the Club. It made for some inspired partnerships: Goran Ivanisevic and Mary Pierce, Mansour Bahrami and Conchita Martinez and Nenad Zimonjic and Marion Bartoli, to name but a few. Oh, to have been a fly on the umpire's chair to listen to some of those conversations at the change of ends.

• Her Majesty The Queen was not the only one celebrating a Platinum Jubilee. Back in Australia, Frank Sedgman was celebrating the 70th anniversary of his trophy triple in 1952: he won the gentlemen's singles, the gentlemen's doubles with fellow Aussie Ken McGregor, and the mixed doubles with Doris Hart from the USA. No one has done it since. Invited to attend The Championships, but unable to make the long journey, 94-year-old Frank, watched this year's Wimbledon unfold from his home in Melbourne, and was honoured with a lunch for 200 guests at Kooyong Lawn Tennis Club, the former home of the Australian Open. Messages of congratulation poured in from around the world, with everyone from Rod Laver to Roger Federer lauding the serve-and-volley master.

Frank's advice for today's players? "You've just got to concentrate and take each match as it comes." Some things never change.

• The Cameron Norrie bandwagon was gathering momentum. The No.9 seed had made his way to his first Grand Slam semi-final. It was time for the renaming of the Hill. When the new No.1 Court was opened in 1997, a giant screen was installed on the side of the stadium just at the bottom of what is officially called Aorangi Terrace. At that time, Tim Henman was the world No.20 and on his way to his second quarter-final in SW19. 'Henmania' was hitting its peak and those with ground passes packed the terrace to watch his exploits on the big screen, and so it became known as 'Henman Hill'. Then Andy Murray arrived on the scene and the faithful renamed the terrace 'Murray Mound'. But what to call it

now? Someone suggested 'Norrie's Knoll' and the proposal was put to the man himself. "I don't even know what a knoll is," he said. "I would say it doesn't roll off the tongue as well as 'Henman Hill'. But, yeah, I'll take it."

Rafael Nadal does not like talking about injury problems during a tournament. At Roland-Garros in June he had not revealed the fact that he had been playing with his left foot numbed by pain-killers until his post-final press conference.

Above: It was clear towards the end of the first set that Rafael Nadal was struggling with an injury, but somehow the Spanish great managed to battle to a five-set victory

Previous pages: Rafael Nadal salutes the Centre Court crowd

On Day Eight of The Championships, meanwhile, an eagle-eyed reporter had asked about the tape on the 36-year-old Spaniard's abdomen during his victory over Botic van de Zandschulp. "I am a little bit tired of talking about my body," Nadal replied. "I prefer not to talk about that now. Sorry for that, but I am in the middle of the tournament and I have to keep going. All respect for the rest of my opponents. I am just trying my best every single day. For the moment I am healthy enough to keep going and fight for the things that I want."

In the early stages of his quarter-final against Taylor Fritz there was little indication that Nadal had any serious physical issues, though the drop in his level as he lost five games in a row to concede the opening set was an indication that something was not right. In the second set, however, it soon became clear that Nadal was struggling. His service speed dropped and there were moments when he was evidently in pain. Leading 4-3, he called for the trainer. As he looked over to his player box, pointing to the taping he was again wearing on the right of his abdomen, he shook his head. Was history repeating

itself, Fritz having won the Indian Wells final in March when Nadal had been troubled by a rib injury? When the No.2 seed left the stadium for a medical time-out his father Sebastian gestured from his player box, urging him to retire.

Minutes later, nevertheless, Nadal was back on court. With Fritz perhaps distracted by what was happening to his opponent, the Spaniard broke serve to take the second set. After Fritz resumed control to win the third set the No.11 seed looked like he was expecting Nadal to retire, but the match continued. Nadal dropped serve twice in the fourth set but broke Fritz three times to take the match into a decider. As the excitement in Centre Court reached fever pitch, Nadal broke serve again to lead 4-3 in the fifth set, only for Fritz to respond in kind. When the match went to a deciding tie-break there was no let-up in the drama. Fritz went 5-0 down before pulling back to 5-3, only for Nadal to win five of the last six points to seal his 3-6, 7-5, 3-6, 7-5, 7-6(4) victory after four hours and 21 minutes.

After one of the most extraordinary victories of Nadal's career, the body language of the two men told its own story. Nadal briefly raised his arms in the air after hitting his match-winning forehand, but clearly knew the price he was paying and barely celebrated. Fritz, who sat in his chair looking utterly disconsolate, later described it as the toughest defeat of his career and said he had felt like crying.

Nadal said afterwards that he had been feeling pain in his abdomen "for a couple of days" and that it had got much worse in the match, during which he needed painkillers and anti-inflammatories. He had considered retiring, but "it's something that I hate to do". What he said was especially frustrating was the fact that he was "playing great". He added: "I just wanted to give myself a chance.

Taylor Fritz came tantalisingly close but ultimately could not find a way to stop his Spanish opponent. "It probably hurts more than any loss I've ever had," he said

Above: Nick Kyrgios was a man on a mission as he overwhelmed Cristian Garin in three sets

Opposite, top: Garin had his chances in the match but was never allowed to take them by his inspired opponent

Opposite, below: Kyrgios falls flat on his back in a mixture of delight and relief as he reaches his first Grand Slam semi-final

Not easy to leave the tournament. Not easy to leave Wimbledon, even if the pain was hard. I wanted to finish. I fought. I'm proud of the fighting spirit and the way that I managed to be competitive under those conditions."

Did Nadal expect to be fit to play again two days later? "Tomorrow I'm going to have some more tests, but it's difficult to know," he said. "I need to know different opinions and I need to check everything the proper way. There is something even more important than winning Wimbledon and that is my health."

By that stage we knew that Nadal was lined up to meet Nick Kyrgios in the semi-finals, the Australian having delivered an emphatic 6-4, 6-3, 7-6(5) victory over Chile's Cristian Garin earlier in the day. The world No.40 would be the lowest-ranked men's semi-finalist at The Championships for 14 years.

Garin had recorded some impressive results en route to his first Grand Slam quarter-final and might have fancied his chances after winning the first nine points on No.1 Court, but he often struggled to deal with Kyrgios' serve. Hitting 17 aces and saving eight of the nine break points he faced, Kyrgios kept his composure for most of the match, though there were times when he yelled at his entourage, demanding more support.

At the end Kyrgios sat in his chair in pensive mood. Asked later what he had been thinking about, he said: "Just how things can change. There was a point where I was almost done with the sport. I posted this year about the kind of mental state I was in in 2019 when I was at the Australian Open, with self-harm and suicidal thoughts and stuff." In his on-court interview Kyrgios admitted: "I never thought I'd be in the semi-final of a Grand Slam. I thought that ship had sailed, that I may have wasted that window in my career."

News had broken the previous day that Kyrgios was due to appear in court in Canberra the following month in relation to an allegation of assault. He said he could not comment on the matter but insisted that it "didn't really affect my preparation at all".

Just as Ons Jabeur had been blazing a trail for Tunisia, so Elena Rybakina continued to fly the flag for Kazakhstan, the country she had represented since 2018. The No.17 seed became the first player representing Kazakhstan to reach a Grand Slam singles semi-final when she recovered from a slow start to beat Ajla Tomljanovic 4-6, 6-2, 6-3. Another Kazakhstani player, Yaroslava Shvedova, had made the quarter-finals at The Championships 2016.

Rybakina said that Kazakhstan's offer to her to change her nationality had come at a good time in her career. "They were looking for the player, I was looking for some help. They believed in me, so I think it was a very good combination. We just found each other." Asked in what way Kazakhstan had helped her, Rybakina said: "They made everything possible for me to keep playing, keep improving. I had all the conditions to practise and everything. Of course, it helped a lot. They are still helping and supporting me."

Calm under pressure, Elena Rybakina recovered from losing the first set to find her range on serve and reach the semi-final

Given her background and the fact that all players representing Russia and Belarus had had their entries for The Championships declined, it was no surprise that Rybakina was asked in her post-match press conference about the conflict in Ukraine. "I just want the war to end as soon as possible," she said.

Did she feel she was Kazakh or Russian? "It's a tough question," Rybakina said. "I was born in Russia, but of course I am representing Kazakhstan. It's already a long journey for me. I was playing Olympics, Fed Cup before. I got so much help and support. I'm feeling just the support of the people and very happy to represent Kazakhstan, because I think I'm also bringing some results, which are very good for the sport in Kazakhstan."

Rybakina's semi-final opponent would be Simona Halep, who needed just 63 minutes to beat Amanda Anisimova 6-2, 6-4 on Centre Court. Anisimova had struck 108 winners – more than any other player in the ladies' singles – in her first four matches but was comprehensively outplayed. The 2019 champion's victory would have been even quicker had Anisimova not won three games in a row from 5-1 down in the second set. While Anisimova said she had felt "stiff and frozen" during the match, Halep enjoyed every moment of her victory. "I'm playing the best tennis since I won

So near but yet so far – Ajla Tomljanovic took the early lead but could not keep pace with her opponent in the latter stages

Simona Halep stretched every sinew and every nerve ending to repel a second set challenge from Amanda Anisimova

here," the Romanian said in her on-court interview. "I'm building that confidence back and it is good right now."

Rajeev Ram and Joe Salisbury, the top seeds in the gentlemen's doubles, came through a tricky quarter-final, beating Nicolas Mahut and Edouard Roger-Vasselin 6-3, 6-7(1), 6-1, 3-6, 6-4 after a Hawk-Eye controversy had threatened to derail them. In the second set Ram and Salisbury thought they had broken serve when a Roger-Vasselin volley was called out, only for Hawk-Eye to reverse the decision. Salisbury's threat to stop playing until Hawk-Eye was turned off was to no avail and he admitted after the match: "I guess there's a chance we all saw it wrong – the line judge, the umpire, us. Maybe we all need to get our eyes checked."

The mixed doubles semi-finals were both hard-fought affairs over three sets. Neal Skupski and Desirae Krawczyk, the defending champions and No.2 seeds, beat Mate Pavic and Sania Mirza, while Matthew Ebden and Sam Stosur, who had knocked out the top seeds Jean-Julien Rojer and Ena Shibahara in the second round, held off Jack Sock and Coco Gauff.

DAILY DIARY DAY 10

Hard though it may be to comprehend, not every eye in Britain was focused on the tennis. Day 10 coincided with the start of the Women's Euros, and 220 miles away at Old Trafford England were taking on Austria to get the tournament under way. Back in SW19, Ons Jabeur (*above*) was preparing for her semi-final against Tatjana Maria but football was never far from her mind. In another life, she admits that she might have been a footballer. "I'm a huge Cristiano Ronaldo fan," she explained. "He's a great athlete and just an inspiration for me." She started playing football aged 10 with her brothers and even now plays at any given opportunity. "Every time I go to Tunisia I try to organise football matches with the tennis players that I know," she said. "And of course, I always wear my favourite Real Madrid shirt and play on the same team as my husband Karim."

• Ajla Tomljanovic's Wimbledon ended in the quarter-finals with her loss to Elena Rybakina – but she will be back. After a year of mixed results, she had reached the last eight at SW19 for the second time. That, she said, was due in no small part to the help of Chris Evert (*above, right*). She often trains at Chris' academy in Florida and the two have become good friends. Even when the former champion was undergoing chemotherapy earlier in the year, she was always at the end of a phone to offer support and encouragement.

"I felt bad at one point," Tomljanovic said. "I remember one time telling her: 'Oh my gosh, I don't want to bother you with my problems because you're doing something way harder.' She's like: 'No, no, I love, in a way, the distraction.' We love each other, so we were there for each other in that way. She texted me before the match that she believes in me and that I need to believe that I belong here." Ajla and Chris will both be back.

• Who watches over the watchmen? The local constabulary, it would seem. Three security guards were allegedly spotted having an altercation after one of them accused another of taking a three-hour lunch break. When the scuffle broke out, one bystander was heard to yell, "Call security!" only for another to answer, "They are security!" Fortunately, the boys in blue were on hand to sort things out.

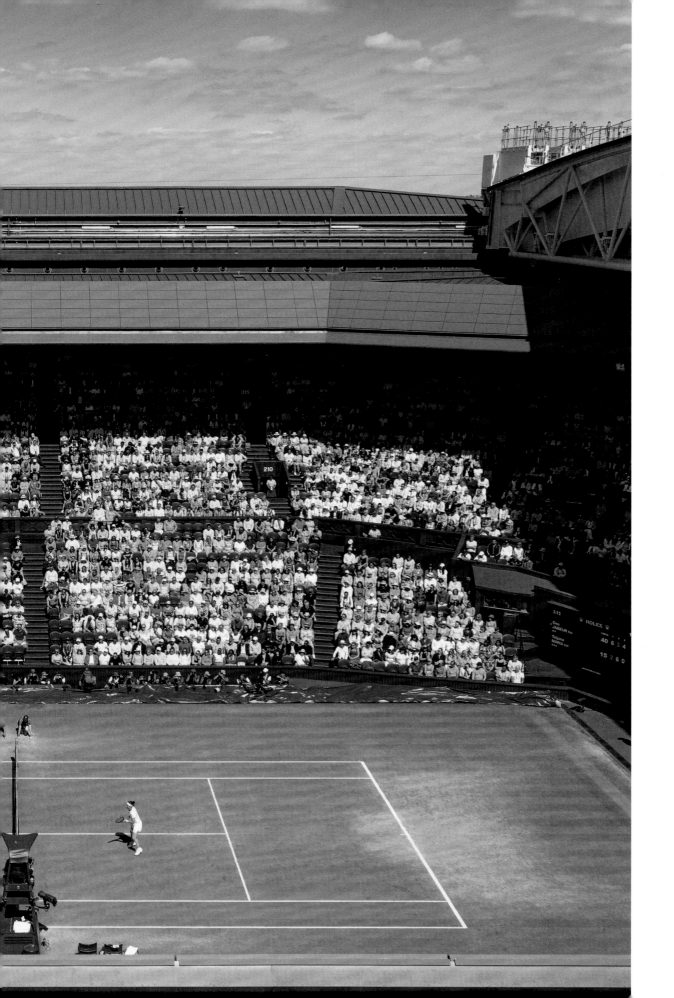

M aking your first appearance on Centre Court can be a nerve-wracking experience for anyone, but what would it be like when you were also making your debut in a Wimbledon semi-final and facing a former champion who was in her best form since her triumph in the same stadium three years earlier? Elena Rybakina was about to find out.

It was probably fair to say that most of the crowd in Centre Court expected Simona Halep to carry the day. The 30-year-old Romanian, who stands just 5ft 6in tall and relies on athleticism rather than pure power, had experience on her side and knew how to handle big hitters like Rybakina. In the 2019 final she had played the match of her life to spike Serena Williams' heavy artillery and in this year's quarter-finals she had left Amanda Anisimova wondering whether she had forgotten to bring her ammunition. Reinvigorated after overcoming injuries and self-doubt over the past year, Halep was relishing every minute of her return to the scene of her greatest achievement. The No.16 seed had won her last 21 sets on the All England Club's courts.

It took just 80 seconds for us to find out how Rybakina would cope with the occasion: the 23-year-old held serve to love after opening up with two service winners and then forcing her opponent into two forehand errors. Halep, double-faulting at deuce in the following game, was soon 0-2 down. Within eight minutes of the start Rybakina, having held serve again, was 3-0 up. Nerves? If there were any, the No.17 seed was shedding them at the speed of some of her 120mph serves.

Halep finally got on the board in the fourth game, but the flow of crunching serves and rasping forehands from Rybakina's racket continued. After losing the first set in 37 minutes, Halep needed to steady the ship in the second, but in the opening game she hit three double faults, including two in a row on the last two points. Romanian hopes rose when Halep levelled the set at 2-2, converting what would be her only break point of the match, but she double-faulted again on break point in the following game. Serving at 3-5 and 40-30, Halep hit her ninth double fault. Two points later Rybakina hit a winning backhand to seal her 6-3, 6-3 victory after just an hour and 16 minutes. The world No.23 admitted later that the only time she had felt nerves had been when she was closing in on victory.

Having won only one match in the two warm-up tournaments she had played on grass before The Championships, Rybakina said she had arrived at the All England Club without any high hopes. "I didn't expect to be here in the second week, especially in the final," she said. "I believe that I have a game to go far in the Grand Slams and of course I believe that maybe one day I can win one, but it was tough because I had injuries. I didn't have a good preparation and it was not a moment when my results were picking up, so of course I came here a bit more relaxed. Maybe this is something that has helped me to get through all these matches."

With Rybakina through to the final, further questions about her Russian background were inevitable at her press conference. Did she still live in Moscow? "Most of the time I spend on tour. I practise in Slovakia between tournaments and I've had camps in Dubai, so I don't live anywhere to be honest." Had she heard from any of the Russian players who were not here? "I'm actually not checking my phone so often." Did she feel like she was representing Kazakhstan? "As I said yesterday, I've been playing for Kazakhstan for a long time. I'm really happy representing Kazakhstan."

Simona Halep needed to be at her absolute best to beat Elena Rybakina – and, as she openly admitted, she wasn't

Ons Jabeur at full
stretch on her way to
winning a stunning
match of slices, dices,
angles and drop shots

ONS-SPIRATIONAL
—

As if trying to reach her first Wimbledon final was not hard enough, Ons Jabeur had set herself another task: to inspire not just the young people in her native Tunisia but across the whole of the continent of Africa and the Middle East.

As the first Arab player, male or female, to reach a Grand Slam singles final – as well as the first African woman not from South Africa to do so – she carried the hopes and dreams of more than 500 million people on her shoulders. But in her cheery way, she carried it lightly.

"I hope, really, I'm trying to inspire the new generation," she said. "We know we have a lot of talented players. We have great tournaments in Tunisia, not just juniors but a lot of other ones. I hope this could push them more to do better and see more players on tour."

The ladies' singles final coincided with the start of Eid al-Adha, her favourite holiday and one that she invariably misses because she is on tour.

"It's like Christmas for you guys," she said. "It always reminds me of being a child. If I make it on that special holiday, it's going to be great."

Her family would not be at the final (they could not get their visas in time), but she would have the crowd with her and was delighted to see so many Tunisians, Arabs and Muslims cheering her on throughout the Fortnight.

"It's amazing to really inspire the new generation," she beamed, "just to show that nothing is impossible really."

Halep said Rybakina had played "really well" and lamented the fact that she had served so poorly ("too many double faults and too soft") but took positives from her grass court season. "I have confidence because I showed myself that I can play good tennis," she said.

Rybakina's opponent in the final would be the No.3 seed, Ons Jabeur, who beat Tatjana Maria, her "barbecue buddy", 6-2, 3-6, 6-1 in the opening match on Centre Court. Maria, who at 34 was the oldest first-time women's Grand Slam semi-finalist in the Open era, showed all the fighting spirit that had already seen her win some tough battles: four of her first five matches had also gone to three sets and she had lost the first set in three of them. However, Jabeur's clever use of drop shots, slices and acute angles proved decisive.

The two women are good friends – Maria's eight-year-old daughter Charlotte calls Jabeur 'Aunt Ons' – and shared a warm embrace at the end. Jabeur then led Maria back into the middle of the court so they could share the crowd's applause. "It was really nice from her that she wanted to celebrate with me, even though it was her moment," Maria said. "She's such a great person. She really deserves it. I'm really happy for her." Maria said she hoped that her own achievement in playing her first Grand Slam semi-final at Wimbledon as a 34-year-old mother of two would send out a message to others that "everything is possible".

As a child Jabeur had never seen a grass court, but said that after playing so well on the surface in 2021, when she reached the Wimbledon quarter-finals, she had told her mental coach: "I'm coming back next year for the title." Jabeur said she loved everything about Wimbledon and had made winning the title here her main goal. She had even imagined herself holding the Venus Rosewater Dish and making a speech as champion. "Now I really need to hold the trophy," she said.

"You are coming with me!" Ons Jabeur points to the middle of the court and insists that Tatjana Maria join her to receive the applause of the crowd

It was the news everyone had feared: an abdominal injury had forced Rafael Nadal to pull out of Wimbledon

Having become the first Tunisian and the first Arab to reach a Grand Slam final, Jabeur said she wanted to "go bigger, inspire many more generations". She explained: "Tunisia is connected to the Arab world, is connected to the African continent. We want to see more players from the area. It's not like Europe or any other countries. I want to see more players from my country, from the Middle East, from Africa. I think we didn't believe enough at a certain point that we could do it. Now I'm just trying to show that. Hopefully people are getting inspired."

On a day of turmoil in British politics following Boris Johnson's resignation as leader of the Conservative Party (and with Sir Keir Starmer, the leader of the opposition Labour Party, in the Royal Box), the conjecture about who would succeed him as Prime Minister was almost matched by the speculation as to whether Rafael Nadal would be fit to play his semi-final against Nick Kyrgios the following afternoon. When the Spaniard practised at Aorangi Park in the afternoon hopes rose, but in the early evening he announced at a media conference that he was withdrawing because of a torn muscle in his abdomen. "I don't think it makes sense to go on," he said. "Even if I tried lot of times during my career to keep going under very tough circumstances, in this case I think it's obvious that if I kept going the injury would get worse and worse."

Nadal said that he had felt a problem in his abdomen for a week but it had become serious in the previous day's quarter-final against Taylor Fritz. "I made my decision because I believe that I can't win two matches under these circumstances," he said. "I can't serve. It's not only that I can't serve at the right speed, because I can't do the normal service motion either."

The main interview room was packed for Rafael Nadal's media conference as the international press sent the breaking news around the world

LET THE WHEELCHAIR GAMES BEGIN!

All eyes were upon Shingo Kunieda (*above*). Could he become the first man to complete a career Grand Slam by winning the Gentlemen's Wheelchair Singles? Alfie Hewett (*below, right*) hoped not – he was chasing the title himself. Diede de Groot (*right*) won the Golden Slam last year and had won the last six major championships prior to her arrival in SW19. The Quad Wheelchair events had been expanded to an eight-strong field this year, with Sam Schroder – the world No.1 – hoping to claim his first Wimbledon title.

Although he had won the first two Grand Slam titles of 2022, Nadal insisted he had never thought about the prospect of winning a calendar-year Grand Slam of the sport's four major titles, which had last been achieved by Rod Laver in 1969.

The day's play on Centre Court ended with the mixed doubles final, which had been moved from its traditional Sunday slot with the aim of giving it a higher profile. It ended in victory for Britain's Neal Skupski and the American Desirae Krawczyk, who became the first pair to win the title in successive years since Cyril Suk and Helena Sukova in 1996 and 1997. Skupski and Krawczyk beat the Australians Matthew Ebden and Sam Stosur 6-4, 6-3.

Skupski revealed afterwards that he had been due to play with Gaby Dabrowski, while Krawczyk had agreed to partner Joe Salisbury. It was only when Salisbury decided not to play mixed doubles that Skupski and Krawczyk got together again. "To try to defend the title with someone you won it with the year before is something I wanted to do personally," Skupski said. "It was very special to do that at Wimbledon."

Ebden was on court for almost five and a half hours in the day, having been involved in a marathon gentlemen's doubles semi-final earlier on alongside Max Purcell. After losing the first two sets to Salisbury and Rajeev Ram, the Australians saved five match points in a tie-break at the end of the third set and went on to win 3-6, 6-7(1), 7-6(9), 6-4, 6-2.

As the Wheelchair events got under way, the highly successful British doubles team of Alfie Hewett and Gordon Reid found themselves on different sides of the net in the singles. After two and a half hours Hewett won a hard-fought contest 6-2, 3-6, 6-4 to earn a semi-final meeting with Argentina's Gustavo Fernandez.

We are the champions! Desirae Krawczyk and Neal Skupski lift the silverware in the mixed doubles after beating Matthew Ebden and Samantha Stosur

DAILY DIARY DAY 11

You have to watch the powers that be at the All England Club: the most proudly traditional of sporting events is apt to come up with a new tradition when you are not looking. This year saw yet more innovation: the addition of 14-and-under events to the Junior Championships (*above*). As Wimbledon is the only one of the four Grand Slams to be played on grass, most of the junior players arrive in SW19 at the age of 17 or 18 having never set foot on the green stuff for a competitive match before. These new events were devised as an opportunity for players to get a feel for the grass at an earlier age. The two 16-player draws included girls and boys from 20 different nations, from as a far afield as New Zealand, Argentina and the Northern Mariana Islands – the latter, an archipelago in the Pacific Ocean with a population of just under 60,000, proudly represented by La Hunn Lam.

• Boris Johnson resigns! Country in crisis! Yes, this was a momentous day as the Prime Minister stepped down, leaving his party to find a new leader and the country to wait for a new PM. As the nation absorbed the news,

Ons Jabeur – who had not only reached the ladies' singles final but had also become the 'go to' person for a decent quote – was asked what she thought of it all. "I have no idea. I'm the Minister of Happiness," she said, beaming broadly. 'The Minister of Happiness' is Jabeur's nickname in Tunisia and is used by everybody, including government ministers. "It's nice of them to call me that," she went on. "The actual Minister always says: 'Hello, Minister'. Hopefully I can keep the title forever."

• Doubles requires teamwork and that sixth sense to know exactly what your partner is going to do. For Mate Pavic and Nikola Mektic, that symbiosis took them to the title here last year, to Olympic gold in Tokyo a few weeks later and, after nine titles in 2021, to the world No.1 ranking. But it was misfiring in the semi-finals against Juan Sebastian Cabal and Robert Farah. The two Croatians headed for the same volley; Pavic got there but smacked his partner in the face with his racket as he did so. As they sat down, Mektic used his phone to check the damage – a split lip – before taking a selfie with his pal and giving him a big hug. And they won, too. All's well that ends well.

After Fred Perry won the last of his three titles in 1936, the British public had to wait 77 years for their next Gentlemen's Singles Champion. Now, just six years after Andy Murray had claimed the All England Club title for a second time, might there be a much shorter wait for the next home hero? Cameron Norrie had enjoyed the best run of his Grand Slam career and now stood within one victory of reaching the Wimbledon final.

Above: Cameron Norrie took the first set but Novak Djokovic, in his inimitable way, reeled him in to win in four

Previous pages: Djokovic was walking on air as he reached his eighth Wimbledon final

The only problem was that the man standing in his way was Novak Djokovic, who had already won the title six times and was now the red-hot favourite to take it again, especially after Rafael Nadal's withdrawal with injury had given Nick Kyrgios a free run to the final in the other half of the draw.

For an hour on a gloriously sunny afternoon on Centre Court the dream of home supporters was very much alive. The man who seemed to be suffering from the most nerves in the opening set was not the Briton playing in his first Grand Slam semi-final but the Serb playing in his 43rd. In the first game Djokovic sprayed the ball around the court, struggling to find his timing, to give Norrie two break points, the second of which the No.9 seed took with a backhand volley. Norrie pumped his fist in celebration, only for Djokovic to break back immediately. However, as Djokovic continued to struggle to find his game the Briton won five games in a row to take the opening set in just 32 minutes. At that stage Djokovic had made 12 unforced errors to Norrie's nine.

There were no breaks in the second set until Norrie served in the eighth game, though Djokovic had been putting increasing pressure on his opponent with the quality of his returns. Serving at 3-4 and 15-40, Norrie had what looked like a routine volley to save the first of two break points but missed it. The break of serve proved to be just the spark that Djokovic needed to light his fire. Finding his range and striking the ball with growing confidence, the defending champion was pushing Norrie further and further back, forcing him on the defensive. Djokovic did not have to defend another break point in the match. After levelling the match by taking the second set, he pressed home his advantage and eventually won 2-6, 6-3, 6-2, 6-4 after two hours and 35 minutes.

Norrie had won only three games in his one previous meeting with Djokovic, as an alternate at the season-ending ATP Finals in 2021, so he had plenty of reasons to feel positive, particularly after pushing the former world No.1 so hard in the early stages. "I think it was a good experience to play him, especially the level he brings here at Wimbledon," Norrie said. "I loved it, loved every moment of it. I think I need to keep working hard. I've still got a lot of things I can improve in my game."

He added: "I want to do more of that and go one further and try to win a Slam. A lot of firsts for me this week, a lot of good experiences. Hopefully I can take them in my stride. Comparing [myself] to Novak, I think it was just the level of execution from him today that was better than me. His level of focus, the way he handled his service games was better than me. That was the difference."

Djokovic, who described Norrie as an "all-round player" and "a very professional guy", sounded relieved to have turned the contest around. "It was a good match," he said. "I didn't start off well as I did in most of my matches here at Wimbledon. I didn't feel so good at the beginning. I made a lot of mistakes and just didn't find my rhythm. Nerves were kicking in for both of us. He handled them better and was a better player for a set and a half.

"The match turned around after one poor game from his side at 4-3 in the second set. I think the momentum shifted. I started feeling better, serving better, just getting him to move around the court, making him work. I played three solid sets after that. I know I always expect that I can play better than I did, but I have to be pleased with this win."

Welcoming the chance to take on Kyrgios in the final two days later, Djokovic spoke highly of the Australian's ability. "Between us players, we've always known how dangerous he is, on grass particularly, because of his game, because of his attitude on the court being so confident, just going for it, being a very complete player," Djokovic said. "It seems like mentally he's in a better state than where he was some years ago. Of course as time passes by you're maturing, you're understanding what you need to do in order to get yourself to the best possible, optimal state of mind, body, and soul in order to perform your best. These are the occasions he loves, where he thrives, on a big stage. So in a way it's also not a surprise for me that he's there.

"Honestly, as a tennis fan, I'm glad that he's in the final because he's got so much talent. Everyone was praising him when he came on the Tour, expecting great things from him. Of course, then we know what was happening for many years with him mentally and emotionally. On and off the court, a lot of different things were distracting him and he was not being able to get this consistency. For the quality player that he is, this is where he needs to be - and he deserves to be."

Above: The Hill was packed as Cameron Norrie sought to become Britain's first singles finalist since Andy Murray in 2016

Opposite: The roar of raw emotion – Novak Djokovic had beaten Britain's No.1 and earned his chance to win his seventh gentlemen's singles title

PUTTING ON A SHOW

—

Who was that mysterious person who kept ringing up Alfie Hewett (*above*) when he was trying to sleep before his Gentlemen's Wheelchair Singles semi-final? As it turned out, it was the Referees' Office trying to tell him that his Friday match had been moved: he and Gustavo Fernandez (*left*) were now first up on No.1 Court.

Hewett had said after his opening match – a three-set thriller – against his friend and doubles partner, Gordon Reid, that he thought the Wheelchair Events should have a bigger stage. A major Show Court, perhaps. And Wimbledon duly obliged. When Rafael Nadal withdrew before his gentlemen's singles semi-final, the schedule had to be reorganised and a slot on that court had become available.

"I was asleep at 9.30pm last night," said Hewlett after winning yet another three-set epic to beat Fernandez, "and I kept getting calls from the Referee. I thought I could ignore it but it was actually a court change. I couldn't get much sleep after that!"

Lack of sleep or not, Hewett came back from a set and 5-1 down to fight his way through to the final. "I've never experienced anything like this before so thank you everyone," he said in his on-court interview. "We've been desperate to showcase our sport in front of a bigger crowd, and I think we showed a pretty good level today."

Just to prove that he could not have too much of a good thing, Hewett – with Reid – was back to No.1 Court a couple of hours later to beat Tom Egberink and Joachim Gerard 6-3, 1-6, 7-6(7) and reach the Gentlemen's Wheelchair Doubles final, too.

Kyrgios, who as world No.40 would be the lowest-ranked Wimbledon men's finalist since his fellow countryman Mark Philippoussis in 2003, was disappointed not to have had the chance to play Nadal in the semi-finals. "You never want to see someone like that, so important to the sport, go down with an injury like that," he said. "We've had a lot of run-ins, a lot of battles. I'm sure at the end of the day everyone did want to see us go to war out there. I hope he just gets better."

As for his opponent in the final, Kyrgios said he and Djokovic had "a bit of a bromance", which he agreed was "weird" given that there had been no love lost between the two men in the past. That had changed in Australia at the start of the year, when Kyrgios was one of the few players to express any sympathy for Djokovic as the Serb went through the process that eventually led to his deportation because he was unvaccinated against Covid.

"I feel like that's where respect is earned," Kyrgios said. "Not on the tennis court, but when a real life crisis is happening and someone stands up for you. We actually message each other on DMs in Instagram now and stuff. It's real weird. Earlier in the week he was like: 'Hopefully I'll see you on Sunday'."

Kyrgios said that he had had only an hour's sleep the night before because he was so excited, having never thought he would have the chance to play for the Wimbledon title. "I feel like it's the pinnacle of tennis," he said. "Once you are able to raise a Grand Slam trophy, what else is there to achieve?"

Nick Kyrgios was in expansive form, covering everything from bromances to history to sleepless nights, as he spoke to the media ahead of the final

Lyudmyla Kichenok from Ukraine and Jelena Ostapenko from Latvia prepare to take on the Czech Republic's Barbora Krejcikova and Katerina Siniakova, in the ladies' doubles semi-final

He said that he had learned much from this year's Australian Open, where he had won the doubles title alongside his compatriot Thanasi Kokkinakis, about how to pace yourself through a Grand Slam tournament, how to rest and practise on days off between matches. "You just have to ride the waves, roll with the punches in a Grand Slam," he said.

With only one gentlemen's singles semi-final played, spectators on Centre Court had the chance to enjoy both ladies' doubles semi-finals. The first featured Barbora Krejcikova and Katerina Siniakova, the No.2 seeds, who were aiming to regain the title they had won in 2018. The Czechs, who have been playing together since they were juniors, had claimed their fourth Grand Slam title at the Australian Open in January and were too strong for Lyudmyla Kichenok and Jelena Ostapenko, winning 6-2, 6-2.

The second semi-final saw Elise Mertens, who had won the title in 2021 alongside Su-Wei Hsieh, and Shuai Zhang take on Desirae Krawczyk, who had won the mixed doubles title the previous evening, and her fellow American, Danielle Collins. Mertens and Zhang, who were the top seeds and stood at No.1 and No.5 respectively in the world rankings, won 6-2, 3-6, 6-3.

DAILY DIARY DAY 12

The Big Apple vibe could not be further removed from Wimbledon's summer garden party atmosphere. Scones with jam and cream? Or a soda and hotdog eaten on the run? You pays your money and you takes your choice. But on Day 12 the tea party came to New York (we will not mention Boston tea parties here for fear of ruffling feathers). In Brooklyn Bridge Park, the famous Hill (be it Henman Hill, Murray Mound or Norrie's Knoll) was recreated for New Yorkers to enjoy the gentlemen's semi-finals and the ladies' and gentlemen's finals over the course of a three-day tennis feast. The park was decorated in Wimbledon's purple and green colours; there were strawberries and cream, chilled gin and tonics and purple petunias at every turn; and the action was shown on a massive screen just like the one in SW19. And all of this with the backdrop of the Manhattan skyline in the distance.

• No matter that Bruno Soares had been knocked out in the third round of the gentleman's doubles; no matter that it was two days later, a time when most defeated seeds would still be licking their wounds (not to mention the fact that he had lost in the second round of the mixed doubles, too); the man from Brazil could not help himself – he is just a huge fan of women's tennis, as he showed when he tweeted: "Women's tennis is in great hands with Iga [Swiatek] and Ons [Jabeur]. Two great human beings and amazing ambassadors for the sport. Being a good human can take you a long way."

• At first, they seem like polar opposites: Lleyton Hewitt (*below*) and Nick Kyrgios. One spent his career as the stereotypical Aussie sportsman – leave everything out on the court; no bragging in victory, no whingeing in defeat. The other… well, suffice to say that Nick has not always followed that code. But as he approached his first Grand Slam final, Nick was singing the praises of his Davis Cup captain who, he felt, was the only Australian former champion who supported him. "Lleyton knows that I kind of do my own thing," he said. "I'm definitely the outcast of the Australian players. He knows to kind of keep his distance and just let me do me. He just sends me a message here or there. That's literally it. Just, 'Well done. Keep going'. Shout-out to Lleyton, I guess." Surely Nick hadn't started another bromance?

CENTRE COURT
SOUTH WEST HALL

In the 138 years since Maud Watson beat her sister Lilian to win the first Ladies' Singles Championship in 1884, players from only 11 different nations had won the title. May Sutton, an American, was the first overseas winner, in 1905, but since then only France, Germany, Australia, Brazil, Spain, Switzerland, the Czech Republic, Russia and Romania had joined the UK and the USA in producing Ladies' Singles Champions.

Above: Ons Jabeur had focused her whole year on this moment – her chance to be crowned champion on Centre Court

Previous pages: Elena Rybakina on the Members' Balcony showing off the Venus Rosewater Dish to the crowd below

Now a 12th country – and an unlikely one at that given Wimbledon's history – would be added to the list. But would it be Elena Rybakina's Kazakhstan or Ons Jabeur's Tunisia?

Just as the number of countries producing Grand Slam winners was expanding, so the net of potential champions was also widening. The achievement of Rybakina and Jabeur meant that the women's finals at the last seven Grand Slam tournaments would have featured 13 different players, with the now retired Ashleigh Barty the only one to have played in more than one of them.

Even by recent standards, Rybakina and Jabeur were particularly inexperienced, neither having previously gone beyond the singles quarter-finals at a Grand Slam event. The last time that two first-time Grand Slam women's singles finalists had met at the All England Club had been in 1962, when Karen Susman beat Vera Sukova. In the Open era only two previous Wimbledon ladies' singles finals had not featured a Grand Slam champion: Jana Novotna against Nathalie Tauziat in 1998 and Marion Bartoli against Sabine Lisicki in 2013.

Both finalists – and Rybakina in particular – might have already made their breakthroughs had it not been for the coronavirus pandemic. Rybakina had reached four finals in the six tournaments she played at the start of 2020 before the sport shut down for nearly five months. It was only the following spring that her career appeared to be back on track as she beat Serena Williams in the fourth round at Roland-Garros, though there were setbacks early in 2022 as she dealt with injury problems and Covid-19.

On a sun-kissed Centre Court the final was a fascinating contrast in styles between Rybakina's raw power and Jabeur's ingenuity. In the first set Jabeur's bewitching combination of drop shots and slices disrupted Rybakina's rhythm as the Tunisian slowed down the rallies. Jabeur, who was handling her opponent's serves with apparent ease, broke in the third game and again in the ninth to take the opening set in 32 minutes.

The No.3 seed had dropped only four points on her own serve in the opening set, but the match turned in the first game of the second as Rybakina broke to 15. The Kazakhstani started to hit her serves and ground strokes with increasing venom and accuracy, while Jabeur's drop shots became less productive as Rybakina chased them down more effectively. The shift in momentum appeared to unsettle Jabeur, who was broken again in the fifth game of the second set after hitting a double fault and making two unforced errors on her forehand from 30-15 up.

The deciding set followed a similar pattern as Rybakina again made an early break. Jabeur had her chances to fight back, but Rybakina successfully defended all seven break points she faced in the second and third sets. The No.17 seed's nerves resurfaced momentarily when she served for the match, but from 15-30 up Jabeur made three successive unforced errors as Rybakina completed her 3-6, 6-2, 6-2 victory.

Above: With power, precision and a quiet determination, Elena Rybakina slowly took control of the final

Following pages: The crowd watches on as Ons Jabeur and Elena Rybakina match each other shot for shot

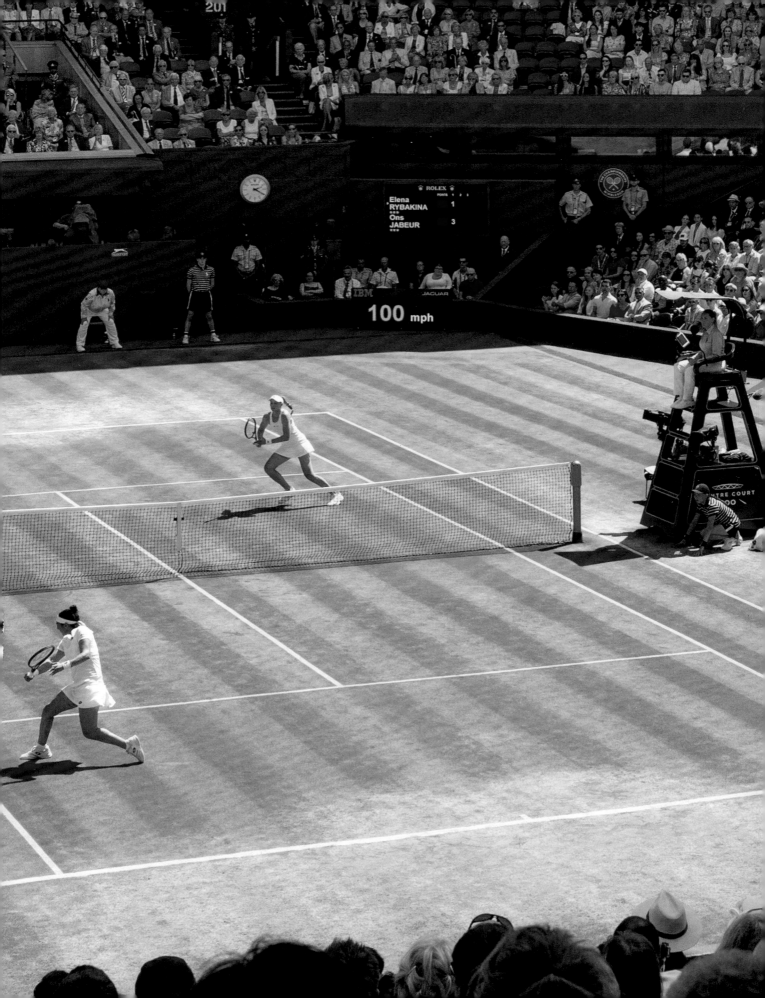

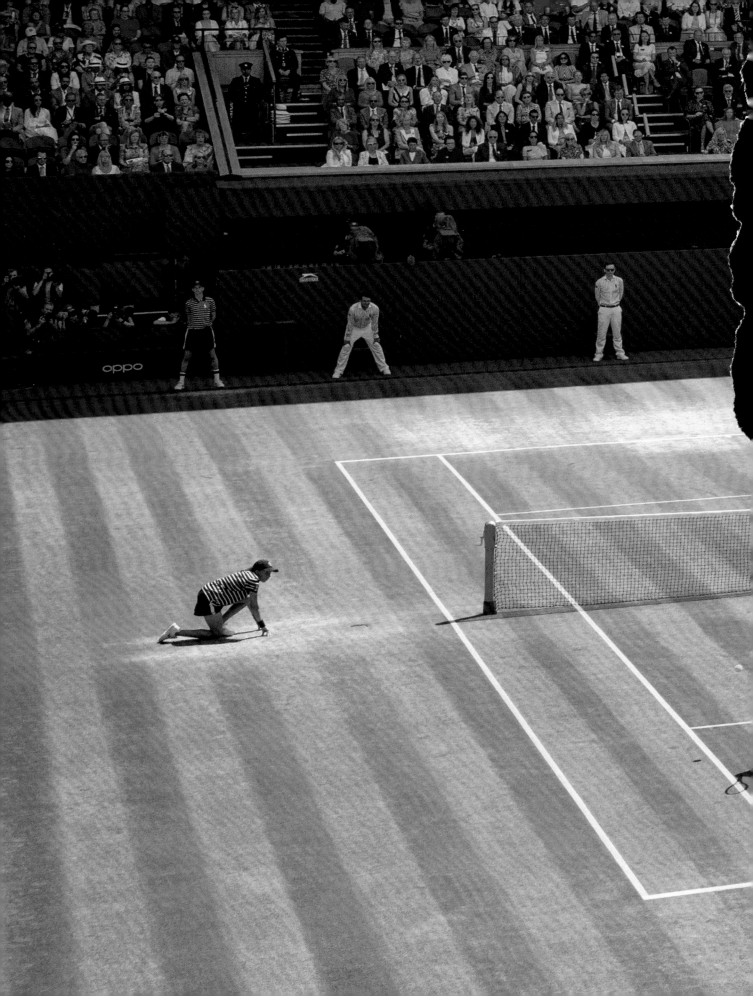

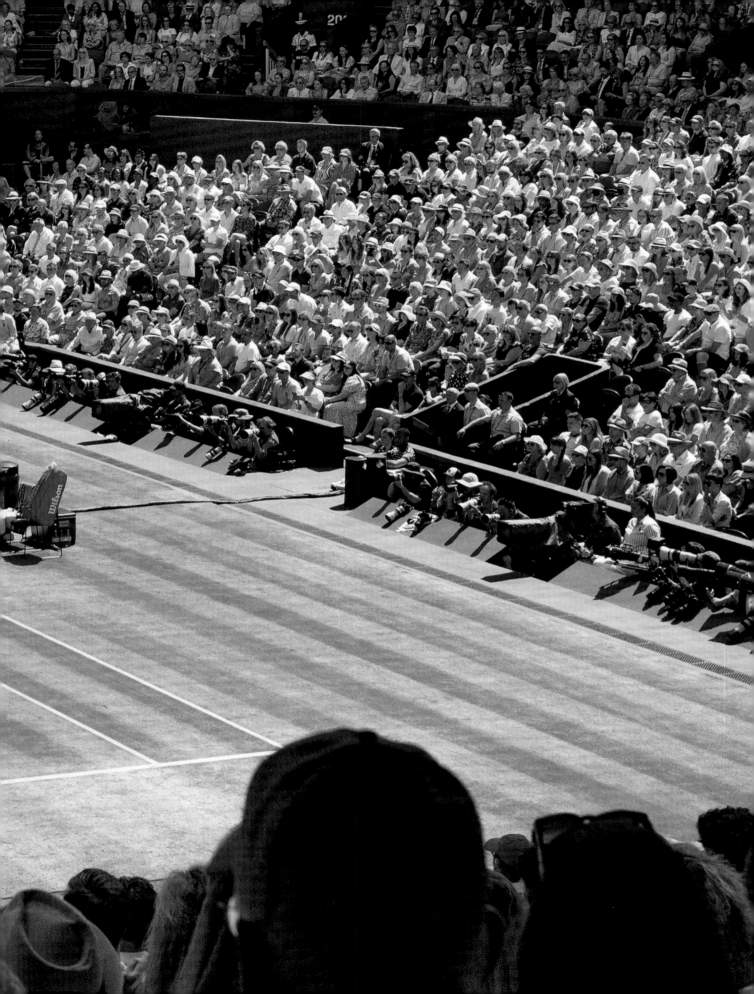

Previous pages:
HRH The Duchess of
Cambridge, patron
of The All England
Club, presents Elena
Rybakina with the
Venus Rosewater Dish

Right: The Duchess
of Cambridge has a
word of consolation
for Ons Jabeur

Opposite: Elena
Rybakina holds the
trophy aloft as the
crowd and the world's
media take their
photographs

Below: One
last photocall for
the players and
their trophies

PERFECT PLATINUM

To mark The Queen's Platinum Jubilee and the Centre Court 100 celebration, The Club commissioned two platinum coins – one for each singles final – with the Centre Court 100 logo on one side and the Platinum Jubilee emblem on the other. The jubilee emblem was designed by Edward Roberts, a 19-year-old graphic design student at Leeds University. He and 13-year-old Gabia Sakaviciute met the Duchess of Cambridge before the ladies' singles final (*above*), while Gabia – who was representing Jigsaw4u – performed the coin toss (*right*).

In only her second main-draw appearance at The Championships, 23-year-old Rybakina had become the youngest winner of the ladies' singles title since Petra Kvitova in 2011. Since the introduction of computer rankings in 1975, Venus Williams, the world No.31 in 2007, was the only lower-ranked player than Rybakina to be crowned champion.

The world No.23 later admitted that she had been nervous in the opening set, but also said she had needed time to adjust to her opponent's game. Jabeur felt she had not been at her best, but also said Rybakina's serving had been crucial. "She played most of the break points really well. I had to accept it. I couldn't do more. I really tried. Deep inside I really tried everything that I could."

As at the end of her previous matches, Rybakina's victory celebrations did not go beyond a brief smile and a clenched fist. "I was just trying to keep myself calm," she said later. "Maybe one day you will see a huge reaction from me, but unfortunately not today." Jabeur said with a smile that she needed to teach Rybakina "how to celebrate really good".

Rybakina said later that she had feared she would cry when speaking during the on-court presentation ceremony, but in the end the only emotion that she showed came towards the end of her post-match media conference, when she was asked what the reaction of her parents would be. "Probably they're going to be super proud," she said as her eyes welled up. "You wanted to see emotion," she added with a tearful laugh. "I kept it [inside] too long."

Growing up in Moscow, Rybakina had started playing tennis at her father's suggestion. Her ability had quickly become evident as she trained at the Spartak Tennis Club in the Russian capital, though

Elena Rybakina and Ian Hewitt, the Chairman of the Club, in front of the ladies' singles honours board

her parents insisted that her education should come first. "I remember that it was so difficult for me to combine tennis and school," Rybakina recalled. "At 17, 18 I had to do my exams at the same time as I was playing in the semi-finals of the French Open juniors. It was a nightmare to be honest: the fights with my parents because they wanted me to study, but at the same time they could see my results as a junior."

Asked whether she now condemned Russia's war in Ukraine, Rybakina said she did not understand the question but added: "I can only say that I'm representing Kazakhstan. I didn't choose where I was born."

The All England Club had declined entries from Russian and Belarusian players on the grounds that it would have been "unacceptable for the Russian regime to derive any benefits from the involvement of Russian or Belarusian players with The Championships". It was therefore no surprise when the Russian Tennis Federation promptly claimed credit for Rybakina's victory. Vladimir Kamelzon, a coach and member of the federation, hailed her triumph as "a stunning victory for Russian tennis" and said Rybakina was "purely Russian" and the product of "a Russian school". Shamil Tarpischev, the federation's president, said: "It turned out that again our country is in favour in London."

Rybakina thanked Bulat Utemuratov, the president of the Kazakhstan Tennis Federation, who has spearheaded the recruitment of players from other countries. "He came to watch and support me from the semis," she said. "He was always on the phone through the weeks, through the matches, supporting me."

The gentlemen's doubles final saw the defending champions, Mate Pavic and Nikola Mektic, denied a second successive Wimbledon title by Matthew Ebden and Max Purcell. The Australians won 7-6(5), 6-7(3), 4-6, 6-4, 7-6(2) in a match that was tight from start to finish. It was remarkable that the Croatian pair went that close given that Pavic, a left-hander, had broken a bone in his right wrist in the semi-finals and had to play with a single-handed backhand.

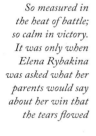

So measured in the heat of battle; so calm in victory. It was only when Elena Rybakina was asked what her parents would say about her win that the tears flowed

MAKING HISTORY FOR KAZAKHSTAN

—

Elena Rybakina's parents may not have been able to be there to see their daughter triumph, but up in the players' box Bulat Utemuratov looked for all the world like a proud father as Kazakhstan gained its first Grand Slam champion.

A multibillionaire businessman and former adviser to the country's president, Utemuratov is – above all else – a tennis fan. He has been at the helm of the Kazakhstan Tennis Federation since 2007 and under his leadership, the sport has grown both at grassroots level and on the international stage. Investing millions of dollars in coaches and indoor facilities, the aim was to have a tennis centre in every city: any child who wanted to play would have access to all they needed.

But encouraging children to play was the problem – tennis was not traditionally a Kazakh sport. What the country needed was role models. If Kazakhstan could have a competitive Davis Cup and Billie Jean King Cup team, watching those players on television could inspire children to play. The offer of financial and practical support for the likes of Rybakina was a gamechanger – especially as Kazakhstan was a former Soviet state, meaning there was no language barrier.

Rybakina switched nationalities in 2018 and now she was the Wimbledon champion. And one of the first people she hugged was Utemuratov. His dream had come true and so had Rybakina's.

Ebden and Purcell made up for their disappointment at losing to Nick Kyrgios and Thanasi Kokkinakis in the Melbourne final six months earlier to claim their first Grand Slam title together and become the first all-Australian team to win Wimbledon since Todd Woodbridge and Mark Woodforde in 2000. Ebden, who had lost in the mixed doubles final two days earlier, said they had practised with Woodforde earlier in the day. "Todd Woodbridge has been chatting with us as well, so we definitely channelled the Woodies," Ebden said. "They are great mentors."

Diede de Groot won her seventh successive Grand Slam title when she beat Yui Kamiji 6-4, 6-2 in the Ladies' Wheelchair Singles Final to take her winning streak to 55 matches. With 15 singles trophies to show from her 21 appearances in Grand Slam events, De Groot moved to within six of her Dutch compatriot Esther Vergeer's record of 21 titles. "I'm getting pretty close, I know this," De Groot said. "But her achievements really stand on their own. For 10 years she wasn't beaten. Those are records that no one's going to beat." Britain's Alfie Hewett and Gordon Reid saw their record-breaking run of 10 successive Grand Slam doubles titles end when they were beaten 3-6, 1-6 by Gustavo Fernandez and Shingo Kunieda in the final.

Liv Hovde, a 16-year-old American, won the girls' singles title by beating Hungary's Luca Udvardy 6-3, 6-4. Hovde, the top seed, said she found grass "a really cool surface to play on" after winning her 12th match in a row on the surface following her victory in the junior ITF warm-up event at Roehampton. She was only the second American girls' singles champion at Wimbledon since 1992. In the girls' doubles Angella Okutoyi became the first Kenyan to win a Grand Slam title when she partnered Rose Marie Nijkamp of the Netherlands to victory over the Canadians Kayla Cross and Victoria Mboko.

The duo from Down Under drop with delight – Matthew Ebden and Max Purcell beat the defending champions from Croatia, Nikola Mektic and Mate Pavic, in the gentlemen's doubles final

DAILY DIARY **DAY 13**

When Ons Jabeur (*above*) first met Elena Rybakina, little could she have imagined that four years later the lady from Kazakhstan would shoulder her aside in the final and snatch away the Venus Rosewater Dish. And Ons had been so nice to her new acquaintance, too. "First time when we met, I went to play maybe one of my first tournaments on the WTA Tour," Rybakina recalled. "I was there with my dad and I didn't even know where is the tennis club, nothing. And I met her. She was super nice to me. She showed [me] everything. That time I was out of the top 200, but she was also not so high in the ranking. It was very nice." Perhaps next time Ons sees a lost soul trying to find her way to the tennis site, she will check with them first before offering them a lift: "Are you planning on beating me in a Wimbledon final in the foreseeable future? No? Fine, get in." Then again, knowing the ever-smiling, ever-happy Ons, perhaps not.

• Meanwhile, Ons had a bit of housekeeping to do. Throughout the Fortnight she had a picture of the Venus Rosewater Dish on the lock screen of her phone. "I did everything since the beginning of the year to really focus on this tournament; I even have the trophy picture on my phone," she said, showing the assembled journalists in the interview room. "But it wasn't meant to

be. Apparently, I should have put the other one [the runner-up's plate]!" But before she could go home, she had to change the picture and restore the photo of her niece to pride of place (family comes first, obviously). As for her general mood, it hadn't changed, despite the result. "Always happy," she smiled. "Like Bob Marley said: 'Don't worry, be happy.'"

• As if there was not enough on the line for the gentlemen's singles final, Nick Kyrgios decided to up the ante. In his new bromance with Novak Djokovic, he had been sparring back and forth with the Serb on social media. "We friends now?" Nick posted. "If you are inviting me for a drink or dinner, I accept. P.S. Winner of

tomorrow [the final] pays," the defending champion replied. "Deal," Kyrgios shot back. "Let's go to a nightclub and go nuts." At that point the conversation came to an abrupt end. Perhaps Jelena Djokovic was sitting at her husband's elbow and did not approve…

"IF YOU CAN MEET WITH TRIUMPH AND DISASTER
AND TREAT THOSE TWO IMPOSTORS JUST THE SAME"

I n contrast to the increasingly wide-open nature of the women's game, men's tennis had continued to be dominated by the old guard. This was despite the fact that two of the so-called 'Big Four' of Roger Federer, Rafael Nadal, Novak Djokovic and Andy Murray were not the forces they used to be.

Above: Novak Djokovic treads a familiar path as he walks out onto Centre Court for his eighth gentlemen's singles final

Previous pages: Nick Kyrgios and Novak Djokovic entranced a capacity crowd with some electric tennis

While Federer and Murray had not won any Grand Slam titles since 2018 and 2016 respectively, Nadal and Djokovic were still the men to beat when it came to challenging for the sport's biggest prizes. Going into The Championships 2022, the Spaniard and the Serb had won 14 of the last 16 Grand Slam titles, while Djokovic's 32nd appearance in a Grand Slam final would be a record among men. Chris Evert (34 finals) and Serena Williams (33) were the only players to have contested more.

At The Championships the supremacy of the older generation has been even more stark. Since Lleyton Hewitt's victory in 2002, the only players who had won the gentlemen's singles title had been Federer, Nadal, Djokovic and Murray. Djokovic, making his 17th consecutive appearance at The Championships, had not lost a match at the All England Club since retiring with an elbow injury in his quarter-final against Tomas Berdych in 2017. He had not lost on Centre Court since Murray beat him in the 2013 final. This would be his eighth gentlemen's singles final; Federer, with 12, was the only man who had played in more.

Nevertheless, going into the 2022 final there were one or two reasons for optimism among Nick Kyrgios' supporters. The 27-year-old Australian had won both his previous meetings with Djokovic, even if they had been more than five years previously. He had also won more Tour-level matches on

grass this year (12) than any other player. Above all, he had proven over the course of the previous two weeks that he had the ability to keep his focus on his tennis over a long period and sustain a high level of performance. When Kyrgios was playing at his absolute best, it was arguable whether anyone in the world could beat him.

A fortnight of fine weather peaked for the final day of The Championships as a blazing sun shone out of a cloudless sky, pushing the temperature towards 29°C. Kyrgios was hot from the start, serving with precision and immediately settling into a groove on his ground strokes. Ever the entertainer, he found time for an underarm serve and a through-the-legs half-volley during a first set which he won in just 31 minutes with a single break of serve in the fifth game after Djokovic had double-faulted at 30-40.

However, no beast in tennis is more dangerous than a wounded Djokovic, who created his first break points after three-quarters of an hour as Kyrgios played a loose game when serving at 1-2 in the second set: with Djokovic getting the measure of the Australian's serve, Kyrgios was unable to handle a potent return on the first point, blazed a wild forehand long on the second and was beaten by a backhand winner into the corner on the third. Djokovic needed only one of his break points, although he was fortunate to see his backhand hit the tape and fall dead on the other side of the net.

Djokovic went 0-40 down when serving for the set, Kyrgios having won a remarkable second point of the game when he chased down a drop shot to hit a spectacular forehand cross-court winner that left the Serb sprawling on the grass. Djokovic, however, served beautifully under pressure, saved four break points in that game and went on to level the match. It proved to be a major turning point as Kyrgios was left to rue his missed opportunities.

Until now the Australian had largely remained focused on his task, but old habits die hard. In the third set he was given a code violation for bad language and complained to the umpire about a spectator

*Resistance is futile.
Novak Djokovic is
the human backboard
– even at full stretch
the ball seemingly
never gets past him*

he said was distracting him. Between points he was chuntering away, complaining about this and that, often, it seemed, to no one in particular. It was the moment Djokovic had been waiting for. As Goran Ivanisevic, the defending champion's coach, said afterwards: "He knew on this stage, when Nick starts to talk, he's going to be vulnerable. That happened."

When Kyrgios dropped his serve in the third set at 4-4 from 40-0 up he appeared to think it was the fault of his entourage because they had momentarily stopped giving him enough vocal backing from his player box. Djokovic served out for the set and took a lengthy bathroom break before the fourth, in which Kyrgios, to his great credit, rediscovered his focus. The set went to a tie-break, which Kyrgios started by double-faulting with a 123mph second serve. Djokovic was soon 6-1 ahead and converted his third match point when he forced Kyrgios into a backhand error. After exactly three hours Djokovic had won 4-6, 6-3, 6-4, 7-6(3) to become the fourth man in the Open era (after Bjorn Borg, Pete Sampras and Federer) to win four or more Wimbledon titles in a row.

After raising his arms to the skies and shaking hands with his opponent, Djokovic, as has become his custom, knelt on the court, picked some blades of grass and put them in his mouth. They clearly tasted as good as ever. The now seven-times champion climbed into the stands and into his player box to embrace his entourage, including his wife, Jelena, on their eighth wedding anniversary. Their four-year-old daughter, Tara, joined in the celebrations, though their seven-year-old son, Stefan, was

playing an important match of his own at that time on one of the practice courts against one of Bob Bryan's sons.

"I've lost words for what this tournament and what this trophy means to me," Djokovic said after receiving the trophy from the Duchess of Cambridge. "It always has been the most special tournament. It was the one that motivated me to play tennis. Every time this tournament gets more special and meaningful."

Kyrgios took plenty of encouragement from his performance. "My level is right there," he said. "I came out in the first set and I looked like I was the one who had played in a lot of finals. I thought I dealt with the pressure pretty well." The Australian also thought the result would benefit him in the future. He explained: "If I had won that Grand Slam title, I think I would have lacked a bit of motivation, to be honest. Coming back for other tournaments, like 250s and stuff, I would have really struggled."

Djokovic admitted at his post-match press conference that the events in the first part of the year, when he had been deported from Australia and was unable to play in the United States because he had chosen to remain unvaccinated against Covid, had affected him badly. "Mentally, emotionally, I was not in a good place," he said. "I just needed time to weather the storm, time to regroup and get into an optimal balanced state on and off the court. My game was there. I know what my qualities are, what my tennis is.

Nick Kyrgios was in full flight in his first Grand Slam final – but it was still not enough to earn him the title

LIKE FATHER, LIKE SON

Sitting between his parents – Their Royal
Highnesses the Duke and Duchess of Cambridge
– HRH Prince George almost stole the show as he
attended his first Wimbledon final (nearly as many
camera lenses were focused on him as were on the
finalists). It was a familiar scene: 31 years before, the
Duke, then aged nine, had accompanied his mother,
Princess Diana, to Wimbledon (*below, right*). Prince
George was clearly enjoying the occasion and if he
follows in his father's footsteps he will catch the
tennis bug – the Duke, together with the Duchess,
is a regular visitor to The Championships.

A champion's joy – with his seventh gentlemen's singles title, Novak Djokovic had equalled the tally of his boyhood hero, Pete Sampras

"It's just all these things off the court that were causing so much distraction and pressure that I had to deal with – not just myself but also people around me. It has been affecting them a lot more probably than me because they've been protecting me. I can feel it through them. It's not one of these things you can switch off and basically pretend that it's not happening. Coming into Wimbledon, I felt good for my tennis because I had won three titles in a row here prior to this year. I always liked playing on grass. I felt like each year I'd been improving."

In winning again, Djokovic became the only man to have won nine Grand Slam singles titles since turning 30. At 35 years and 49 days he was also the second-oldest Gentlemen's Singles Champion in the Open era behind Federer, who was 35 years and 342 days when he claimed his record eighth title in 2017. A seventh triumph put Djokovic in second place on the all-time list of Gentlemens' Singles Champions alongside Sampras and William Renshaw. Meanwhile his tally of Grand Slam singles titles now stood at 21, one behind Nadal and one ahead of Federer.

Although uncertainty hung over his participation in the next two Grand Slam events in New York and Melbourne because of continuing Covid issues, Djokovic suggested that he still had time on his side in his quest to break more records. "I don't feel I'm in a rush anywhere to end my career in a year or two or whenever," he said. "I'm not thinking about it. I want to keep my body healthy because that's obviously necessary in order to keep going at this level. Of course [I need to] keep myself mentally sane and motivated to compete with the young guns."

Within seconds of match point (and with a rock-steady hand), the engraver records the new champion's name on the trophy. He has had plenty of practice with this particular champion, though – this was Novak Djokovic's fourth consecutive title

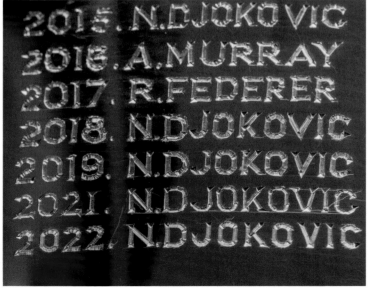

Left: Back in safe hands – Novak Djokovic holds the trophy that has been his since 2018

Following pages: The Ball Boys and Girls form a guard of honour for the champion and the runner-up

The concluding match on Centre Court saw Barbora Krejcikova and Katerina Siniakova claim the ladies' doubles title for the second time following their victory in 2018. The No.2 seeds, who had also won the girls' doubles title in 2013, beat Elise Mertens and Shuai Zhang, the top seeds, 6-2, 6-4. Krejcikova and Siniakova took the first set in just over half an hour after breaking Zhang's serve in the second game and her partner's in the eighth. Mertens and Zhang, who had played only two previous events together, broke Siniakova in the seventh game of the second set to lead 4-3 but won only one more point thereafter as the Czechs sealed their victory in just 66 minutes.

It was a fifth Grand Slam doubles triumph for Krejcikova and Siniakova, who had also won the Olympic title in Tokyo the previous summer. "We really like to play on a big court, so I think we really enjoyed the atmosphere," Krejcikova said afterwards. "From the very first point we really, really wanted to win. I'm really proud of us, that we managed to do that and that we get another trophy."

Winning Grand Slam trophies is a familiar experience for Shingo Kunieda, but in beating Alfie Hewett 4-6, 7-5, 7-6(5) in the Gentlemen's Wheelchair Singles Final the 38-year-old claimed his first Wimbledon singles title. Kunieda went into the final seeking his 28th Grand Slam singles title but had played in only one previous final at The Championships, losing to Gustavo Fernandez in 2019. Hewett, who was also seeking his first Wimbledon singles title, had won a marathon semi-final against Fernandez and was drawn into another epic, but the 24-year-old Briton was edged out in a deciding tie-break after three hours and 20 minutes.

Kunieda became the first men's Wheelchair player to complete a career Grand Slam in singles. Already the holder of the US Open, Australian Open and Roland-Garros titles, he could also celebrate

a so-called 'Golden Slam', having won the Olympic title in his home country the previous summer. "I really wanted to get this title," Kunieda said. "You know my age, 38, so I was thinking it would be my last chance today."

Mili Poljicak, aged 17, became the first player from Croatia to win the boys' 18&U singles title when he held off Michael Zheng, of the United States, in a hard-fought final on No.1 Court. Poljicak, who had warmed up in the morning by practising with Djokovic, won 7-6(2), 7-6(3) after nearly two hours. Se Hyuk Cho and Alexia Ioana Tatu were crowned champions in the inaugural boys' and girls' 14-and-under events respectively.

A memorable Championships was brought to a close that evening at the Champions' Dinner, which was held for the first time in a marquee in Wimbledon Park across the road from Centre Court. Ian Hewitt, the All England Club's Chairman, told the guests that it had been a Wimbledon Fortnight of many firsts, including the first scheduled play on Middle Sunday and the first 14-and-under Junior event. "This year has been extra special," he said. "To be able to stage The Championships with full capacity and without any Covid restrictions has been a real joy after three troubled years. The standard of play, the competitiveness and the excitement of the matches has been fantastic throughout this Fortnight."

For all concerned the only disappointment was that we would have to wait 50 weeks to enjoy it all again.

Previous pages:
Novak Djokovic
salutes the cheering
crowd from the
Members' Balcony

Below: The
champions of the
new 14&U event:
Alexia Ioana Tatu
of Romania (left)
and Se Hyuk Cho
of Korea

DAILY DIARY DAY 14

In the world of television – and professional sport for that matter – timing is everything. And in her 30 years as the face and voice of Wimbledon, Sue Barker's (*above*) timing has been immaculate. She has guided tearful champions (Roger Federer) and runners-up (Andy Murray) through their on-court interviews; she has kept the BBC viewers up to speed with events around the Grounds and she has interviewed countless guests in the studio, coaxing out of them jovial anecdotes and nuggets of wisdom. Now, in Her Majesty The Queen's Platinum Jubilee year – as well as Centre Court's centenary – the timing was perfect: she was hanging up her microphone for good. But not before making sure everything was just as it should be. As she interviewed Novak Djokovic she made sure that the now seven-times champion had remembered just what this day was all about – it was his eighth wedding anniversary and his wife was sitting in the players' box. Novak laughed nervously. He wished his wife a happy anniversary before turning to Sue and saying with some thanks: "I'm going to buy you flowers after this!" And then she was gone. Wimbledon won't be quite the same without her.

• If anyone is missing a budgie, could they please let the All England Club know. One of the gardeners was hard at work primping the pansies and polishing the petunias in the players' area when he spotted a stray budgie. Rather than shoo it away (the easy option) he carefully caught it and found somewhere safe for it to stay. But whose was it and what to do now? Budgies don't come with name tags and lost property didn't have the facilities for misplaced feathered things. When last we heard the search for the owner was ongoing.

• They said they were going to bring Wimbledon to New York – and they did. Even down to the Queue. Nobody queues quite like the British (at a push, we can form a queue in an empty field) but before the gentlemen's singles final was shown in Brooklyn Bridge Park, there were the New Yorkers forming an orderly

line as they waited their turn to claim a space on the relocated Hill. Who knows – by this time next year they may even have learned how to make a decent cup of tea? Such is the power of Wimbledon...

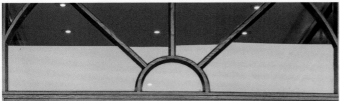

YOU SHALL GO TO THE BALL

At last it was time to relax: the hard work was over, the pressure had been released and now it was off to celebrate their achievements at the Champions' Dinner, held across the road in Wimbledon Park. *Clockwise from left:* Elena Rybakina was obviously in party mood; Ian Hewitt, Chairman of the AELTC, and his wife, Jenifer, on their way to the festivities; Novak and Jelena Djokovic pose in the doorway to the clubhouse. *Opposite page, clockwise from top:* Todd Woodbridge interviews Novak Djokovic; Elena Rybakina raises a glass with her friends; singers provide the evening's entertainment; Shingo Kunieda enjoys the festivities and Todd Woodbridge interviews Elena Rybakina.

CHAMPION FAMILY TIME

For once, the 'Keep Off The Grass' sign that sits on Centre Court for 49 weeks of the year had been removed. Novak Djokovic, his wife Jelena and their children, Stefan and Tara, were allowed to have their photographs taken with the trophy on the aforementioned grass on the Monday after the final – and Stefan (aged seven) and Tara (four) were allowed to have a bit of fun. Stefan was clearly in the mood to let off some steam; Tara just wanted Dad to give her a piggyback. Later the happy family were joined by a group of young tennis players for a final photo.

WIMBLEDON 2022

—

THE GENTLEMEN'S SINGLES
Novak DJOKOVIC

THE LADIES' SINGLES
Elena RYBAKINA

THE GENTLEMEN'S DOUBLES
Matthew EBDEN
Max PURCELL

THE LADIES' DOUBLES
Katerina SINIAKOVA
Barbora KREJCIKOVA

THE MIXED DOUBLES
Neal SKUPSKI
Desirae KRAWCZYK

THE GENTLEMEN'S
WHEELCHAIR SINGLES
Shingo KUNIEDA

THE LADIES'
WHEELCHAIR SINGLES
Diede DE GROOT

THE GENTLEMEN'S
WHEELCHAIR DOUBLES
Gustavo FERNANDEZ
Shingo KUNIEDA

THE LADIES'
WHEELCHAIR DOUBLES
Yui KAMIJI
Dana MATHEWSON

THE CHAMPIONS

—

THE QUAD
WHEELCHAIR SINGLES

Sam SCHRODER

THE QUAD
WHEELCHAIR DOUBLES

**Sam SCHRODER
Niels VINK**

THE 18&U BOYS'
SINGLES

Mili POLJICAK

THE 18&U GIRLS'
SINGLES

Liv HOVDE

THE 18&U BOYS' DOUBLES

**Sebastian GORZNY
Alex MICHELSEN**

THE 18&U GIRLS' DOUBLES

**Angella OKUTOYI
Rose Marie NIJKAMP**

THE 14&U BOYS'
SINGLES

Se Hyuk CHO

THE 14&U GIRLS'
SINGLES

Alexia Ioana TATU

THE GENTLEMEN'S
INVITATION DOUBLES

**Bob BRYAN
Mike BRYAN**

THE LADIES'
INVITATION DOUBLES

**Kim CLIJSTERS
Martina HINGIS**

THE MIXED
INVITATION DOUBLES

**Marion BARTOLI
Nenad ZIMONJIC**

THE GENTLEMEN'S SINGLES CHAMPIONSHIP 2022
Holder: NOVAK DJOKOVIC (SRB)

The Champion will become the holder, for the year only, of the CHALLENGE CUP. The Champion will receive a silver three-quarter size replica of the Challenge Cup. A Silver Salver will be presented to the Runner-up and a Bronze Medal to each defeated semi-finalist.
The matches will be the best of five sets. If the score should reach 6-6 in the final set, the match will be decided by a first-to-ten tie-break.

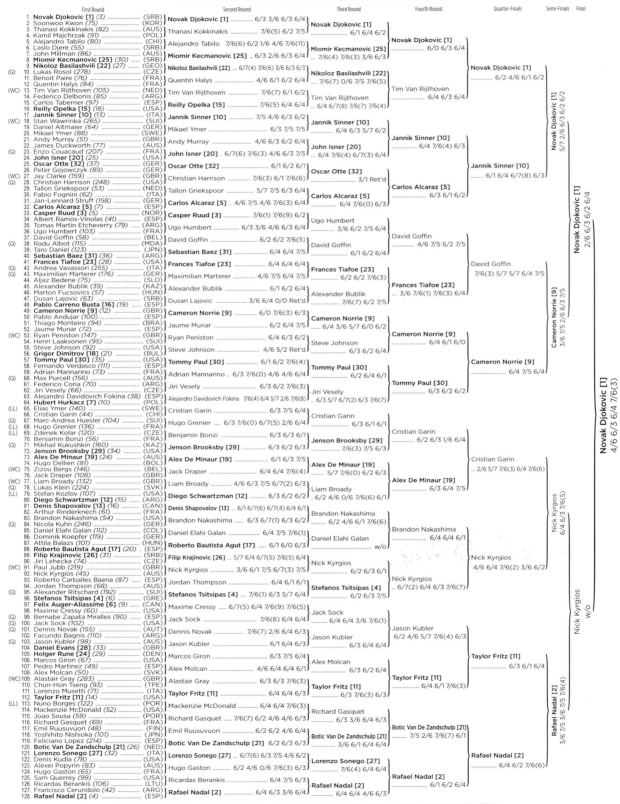

First Round / Second Round / Third Round / Fourth Round / Quarter-Finals / Semi-Finals / Final

1. **Novak Djokovic [1]** *(3)* .... (SRB)
2. Soonwoo Kwon *(75)* .... (KOR)
3. Thanasi Kokkinakis *(82)* .... (AUS)
4. Kamil Majchrzak *(91)* .... (POL)
5. Alejandro Tabilo *(80)* .... (CHI)
6. Laslo Djere *(55)* .... (SRB)
7. John Millman *(86)* .... (AUS)
8. **Miomir Kecmanovic [25]** *(30)* .... (SRB)
9. **Nikoloz Basilashvili [22]** *(27)* .... (GEO)
(Q) 10. Lukas Rosol *(278)* .... (CZE)
11. Benoit Paire *(76)* .... (FRA)
12. Quentin Halys *(84)* .... (FRA)
(WC) 13. Tim Van Rijthoven *(105)* .... (NED)
14. Federico Delbonis *(85)* .... (ARG)
15. Carlos Taberner *(97)* .... (ESP)
16. **Reilly Opelka [15]** *(18)* .... (USA)
17. **Jannik Sinner [10]** *(13)* .... (ITA)
(WC) 18. Stan Wawrinka *(265)* .... (SUI)
19. Daniel Altmaier *(64)* .... (GER)
20. Mikael Ymer *(88)* .... (SWE)
21. Andy Murray *(51)* .... (GBR)
22. James Duckworth *(77)* .... (AUS)
(Q) 23. Enzo Couacaud *(207)* .... (FRA)
24. **John Isner [20]** *(25)* .... (USA)
25. **Oscar Otte [32]** *(37)* .... (GER)
26. Peter Gojowczyk *(89)* .... (GER)
(WC) 27. Jay Clarke *(159)* .... (GBR)
(Q) 28. Christian Harrison *(248)* .... (USA)
29. Tallon Griekspoor *(53)* .... (NED)
30. Fabio Fognini *(62)* .... (ITA)
31. Jan-Lennard Struff *(158)* .... (GER)
32. **Carlos Alcaraz [5]** *(7)* .... (ESP)
33. **Casper Ruud [3]** *(5)* .... (NOR)
34. Albert Ramos-Vinolas *(41)* .... (ESP)
35. Tomas Martin Etcheverry *(79)* .... (ARG)
36. Ugo Humbert *(103)* .... (FRA)
37. David Goffin *(58)* .... (BEL)
(Q) 38. Radu Albot *(115)* .... (MDA)
39. Taro Daniel *(123)* .... (JPN)
40. **Sebastian Baez [31]** *(36)* .... (ARG)
41. **Frances Tiafoe [23]** *(28)* .... (USA)
(Q) 42. Andrea Vavassori *(255)* .... (ITA)
(Q) 43. Maximilian Marterer *(176)* .... (GER)
44. Aljaz Bedene *(75)* .... (SLO)
45. Alexander Bublik *(39)* .... (KAZ)
46. Marton Fucsovics *(57)* .... (HUN)
47. Dusan Lajovic *(63)* .... (SRB)
48. **Pablo Carreno Busta [16]** *(19)* .... (ESP)
49. **Cameron Norrie [9]** *(12)* .... (GBR)
50. Pablo Andujar *(100)* .... (ESP)
51. Thiago Monteiro *(94)* .... (BRA)
52. Jaume Munar *(72)* .... (ESP)
(WC) 53. Ryan Peniston *(147)* .... (GBR)
54. Henri Laaksonen *(95)* .... (SUI)
55. Steve Johnson *(92)* .... (USA)
56. **Grigor Dimitrov [18]** *(21)* .... (BUL)
57. **Tommy Paul [30]** *(35)* .... (USA)
58. Fernando Verdasco *(111)* .... (ESP)
59. Adrian Mannarino *(73)* .... (FRA)
(Q) 60. Max Purcell *(156)* .... (AUS)
61. Federico Coria *(70)* .... (ARG)
62. Jiri Vesely *(66)* .... (CZE)
63. Alejandro Davidovich Fokina *(38)* .... (ESP)
64. **Hubert Hurkacz [7]** *(10)* .... (POL)
(LL) 65. Elias Ymer *(140)* .... (SWE)
(Q) 66. Cristian Garin *(44)* .... (CHI)
(Q) 67. Marc-Andrea Huesler *(104)* .... (SUI)
(LL) 68. Hugo Grenier *(136)* .... (FRA)
(LL) 69. Zdenek Kolar *(120)* .... (CZE)
70. Benjamin Bonzi *(56)* .... (FRA)
(Q) 71. Mikhail Kukushkin *(160)* .... (KAZ)
72. **Jenson Brooksby [29]** *(34)* .... (USA)
73. **Alex De Minaur [19]** *(24)* .... (AUS)
74. Hugo Dellien *(81)* .... (BOL)
(WC) 75. Zizou Bergs *(146)* .... (BEL)
76. Jack Draper *(108)* .... (GBR)
(WC) 77. Liam Broady *(132)* .... (GBR)
(Q) 78. Lukas Klein *(224)* .... (SVK)
(LL) 79. Stefan Kozlov *(107)* .... (USA)
80. **Diego Schwartzman [12]** *(15)* .... (ARG)
81. **Denis Shapovalov [13]** *(16)* .... (CAN)
82. Arthur Rinderknech *(61)* .... (FRA)
83. Brandon Nakashima *(54)* .... (USA)
(Q) 84. Nicola Kuhn *(246)* .... (GER)
85. Daniel Elahi Galan *(112)* .... (COL)
86. Dominik Koepfer *(119)* .... (GER)
87. Attila Balazs *(101)* .... (HUN)
88. **Roberto Bautista Agut [17]** *(20)* .... (ESP)
89. **Filip Krajinovic [26]** *(31)* .... (SRB)
90. Jiri Lehecka *(74)* .... (CZE)
(WC) 91. Paul Jubb *(219)* .... (GBR)
92. Nick Kyrgios *(45)* .... (AUS)
93. Roberto Carballes Baena *(87)* .... (ESP)
94. Jordan Thompson *(68)* .... (AUS)
(Q) 95. Alexander Ritschard *(192)* .... (SUI)
96. **Stefanos Tsitsipas [4]** *(6)* .... (GRE)
97. **Felix Auger-Aliassime [6]** *(9)* .... (CAN)
98. Maxime Cressy *(60)* .... (USA)
(Q) 99. Bernabe Zapata Miralles *(90)* .... (ESP)
(Q) 100. Jack Sock *(102)* .... (USA)
(Q) 101. Dennis Novak *(155)* .... (AUT)
102. Facundo Bagnis *(110)* .... (ARG)
(Q) 103. Jason Kubler *(103)* .... (AUS)
104. **Daniel Evans [28]** *(33)* .... (GBR)
105. **Holger Rune [24]** *(29)* .... (DEN)
106. Marcos Giron *(67)* .... (USA)
107. Pedro Martinez *(49)* .... (ESP)
108. Alex Molcan *(50)* .... (SVK)
(WC) 109. Alastair Gray *(283)* .... (GBR)
110. Chun-Hsin Tseng *(93)* .... (TPE)
111. Lorenzo Musetti *(71)* .... (ITA)
112. **Taylor Fritz [11]** *(14)* .... (USA)
(LL) 113. Nuno Borges *(122)* .... (POR)
114. Mackenzie McDonald *(52)* .... (USA)
115. Joao Sousa *(59)* .... (POR)
116. Richard Gasquet *(69)* .... (FRA)
117. Emil Ruusuvuori *(48)* .... (FIN)
118. Yoshihito Nishioka *(101)* .... (JPN)
119. Feliciano Lopez *(214)* .... (ESP)
120. **Botic Van De Zandschulp [21]** *(26)* .... (NED)
121. **Lorenzo Sonego [27]** *(32)* .... (ITA)
122. Denis Kudla *(78)* .... (USA)
123. Alexei Popyrin *(83)* .... (AUS)
124. Hugo Gaston *(65)* .... (FRA)
125. Sam Querrey *(99)* .... (USA)
126. Ricardas Berankis *(106)* .... (LTU)
127. Francisco Cerundolo *(42)* .... (ARG)
128. **Rafael Nadal [2]** *(4)* .... (ESP)

Second Round

Novak Djokovic [1] — 6/3 3/6 6/3 6/4
Thanasi Kokkinakis — 7/6(5) 6/2 7/5
Alejandro Tabilo — 7/6(6) 6/2 1/6 4/6 7/6(11)
Miomir Kecmanovic [25] — 6/3 2/6 6/3 6/4
Nikoloz Basilashvili [22] — 6/7(4) 7/6(6) 3/6 6/3 6/3
Quentin Halys — 4/6 6/1 6/2 6/4
Tim Van Rijthoven — 7/6(7) 6/1 6/2
Jannik Sinner [10] — 7/5 4/6 6/3 6/2
Mikael Ymer — 6/3 7/5 7/5
Andy Murray — 4/6 6/3 6/2 6/4
John Isner [20] — 6/7(6) 7/6(3) 4/6 6/3 7/5
Oscar Otte [32] — 6/1 6/2 6/1
Christian Harrison — 7/6(3) 6/1 7/6(6)
Tallon Griekspoor — 5/7 7/6(5) 6/4
Carlos Alcaraz [5] — 4/6 5/7 4/6 7/6(3) 6/4
Casper Ruud [3] — 7/6(1) 7/6(9) 6/2
Ugo Humbert — 6/3 3/6 4/6 6/3 6/4
David Goffin — 6/2 6/2 7/6(5)
Sebastian Baez [31] — 6/4 6/4 7/5
Frances Tiafoe [23] — 6/4 6/4 6/4
Maximilian Marterer — 4/6 7/5 6/4 7/5
Alexander Bublik — 6/1 6/2 6/4
Dusan Lajovic — 3/6 6/4 0/0 Ret'd
Cameron Norrie [9] — 6/0 7/6(3) 6/3
Jaume Munar — 6/2 6/4 7/5
Ryan Peniston — 6/4 6/3 6/2
Steve Johnson — 4/6 5/2 Ret'd
Tommy Paul [30] — 6/1 6/2 7/6(4)
Adrian Mannarino — 6/3 7/6(0) 4/6 4/6 6/4
Jiri Vesely — 6/3 6/1 6/3
Alejandro Davidovich Fokina — 7/6(4) 6/4 5/7 2/6 7/6(8)
Cristian Garin — 6/3 7/6(3) 6/4
Hugo Grenier — 6/3 7/6(0) 6/7(5) 2/6 6/4
Benjamin Bonzi — 6/3 6/3 6/1
Jenson Brooksby [29] — 6/3 6/2 6/3
Alex De Minaur [19] — 6/1 6/3 7/5
Jack Draper — 6/4 6/4 7/6(4)
Liam Broady — 4/6 6/3 7/5 6/7(2) 6/3
Diego Schwartzman [12] — 7/6(1) 6/3 5/7 6/4
Denis Shapovalov [13] — 6/1 6/7(6) 7/6(4) 6/4 6/1
Brandon Nakashima — 6/3 6/7(1) 6/3 6/2
Daniel Elahi Galan — 6/4 7/5 7/6(1)
Roberto Bautista Agut [17] — 6/1 6/0 6/3
Filip Krajinovic [26] — 5/7 6/4 6/7(5) 7/6(5) 6/4
Nick Kyrgios — 3/6 6/1 7/5 6/7(3) 7/5
Jordan Thompson —
Stefanos Tsitsipas [4] — 7/6(1) 6/3 5/7 6/4
Maxime Cressy — 6/7(5) 6/4 7/6(9) 7/6(5)
Jack Sock — 7/6(6) 6/4 6/4
Dennis Novak — 7/6(7) 2/6 6/4 6/3
Jason Kubler — 6/1 6/4 6/3
Marcos Giron — 6/3 7/5 6/4
Alex Molcan — 4/6 6/4 6/4 6/1
Alastair Gray — 6/3 6/3 7/6(3)
Taylor Fritz [11] —
Mackenzie McDonald — 6/4 6/4 7/6(3)
Richard Gasquet — 7/6(7) 6/2 4/6 4/6 6/3
Emil Ruusuvuori — 6/2 6/2 4/6 6/4
Botic Van De Zandschulp [21] — 6/2 6/3 6/3
Lorenzo Sonego [27] — 6/7(6) 6/3 7/5 4/6 6/2
Hugo Gaston — 6/2 4/6 0/6 7/6(3) 6/3
Ricardas Berankis — 6/4 7/5 6/3
Rafael Nadal [2] — 6/4 6/3 3/6 6/4

Third Round

Novak Djokovic [1] — 6/1 6/4 6/2
Miomir Kecmanovic [25] — 7/6(4) 7/6(3) 3/6 6/3
Nikoloz Basilashvili [22] — 7/6(7) 0/6 7/5 7/6(5)
Tim Van Rijthoven — 6/4 6/3 6/4
Jannik Sinner [10] — 6/4 6/3 5/7 6/2
John Isner [20] — 6/4 7/6(4) 6/7(3) 6/4
Oscar Otte [32] — 3/1 Ret'd
Carlos Alcaraz [5] — 6/3 6/1 6/2
Ugo Humbert — 3/6 6/2 7/5 6/4
David Goffin — 6/1 6/2 6/4
Frances Tiafoe [23] — 6/2 6/2 7/6(3)
Alexander Bublik — 7/6(7) 6/2 7/5
Cameron Norrie [9] — 6/4 3/6 6/2 6/0
Steve Johnson — 6/3 6/2 6/4
Tommy Paul [30] — 6/2 6/4 6/1
Jiri Vesely — 6/3 5/7 7/6(2) 6/3 7/6(7)
Cristian Garin — 6/3 6/1 6/1
Jenson Brooksby [29] — 7/6(3) 7/5 6/3
Alex De Minaur [19] — 5/7 7/6(0) 6/2 6/3
Liam Broady — 6/2 4/6 0/6 7/6(3) 6/1
Brandon Nakashima — 6/2 4/6 6/1 7/6(6)
Daniel Elahi Galan — w/o
Nick Kyrgios — 6/2 6/3 6/1
Stefanos Tsitsipas [4] — 6/2 6/3 7/5
Jack Sock — 6/4 6/4 3/6 7/6(1)
Jason Kubler — 6/3 6/2 6/4
Alex Molcan — 6/3 6/2 6/4
Taylor Fritz [11] — 6/3 7/6(3) 6/3
Richard Gasquet —
Botic Van De Zandschulp [21] — 3/6 6/4 6/4
Lorenzo Sonego [27] — 7/6(4) 6/4 6/4
Rafael Nadal [2] — 6/4 6/4 4/6 6/3

Fourth Round

Novak Djokovic [1] — 6/0 6/3 6/4
Nikoloz Basilashvili [22] — 7/6(4) 7/6(3) 3/6 6/3
Jannik Sinner [10] — 6/4 7/6(4) 6/3
Carlos Alcaraz [5] — 6/3 6/1 6/2
David Goffin — 3/6 6/2 7/5 6/4
Frances Tiafoe [23] — 3/6 7/6(1) 7/6(3) 6/4
Cameron Norrie [9] — 6/4 6/1 6/0
Tommy Paul [30] — 6/3 6/2 6/2
Cristian Garin — 6/2 6/3 1/6 6/4
Alex De Minaur [19] — 6/3 6/4 7/5
Brandon Nakashima — 6/4 6/4 6/1
Nick Kyrgios — 6/7(2) 4/6 6/3 7/6(7)
Jason Kubler — 6/2 4/6 5/7 7/6(4) 6/3
Taylor Fritz [11] — 6/4 6/1 7/6(3)
Botic Van De Zandschulp [21] — 7/5 2/6 7/6(7) 6/1
Rafael Nadal [2] — 6/1 6/2 6/4

Quarter-Finals

Novak Djokovic [1] — 6/2 4/6 6/1 6/2
Jannik Sinner [10] — 6/1 6/4 6/7(8) 6/3
David Goffin — 7/6(3) 5/7 5/7 6/4 7/5
Cameron Norrie [9] — 6/4 7/5 6/4
Cristian Garin — 2/6 5/7 7/6(3) 6/4 7/6(6)
Nick Kyrgios — 4/6 6/4 7/6(2) 3/6 6/2
Taylor Fritz [11] —
Rafael Nadal [2] — 3/6 7/5 3/6 7/5 7/6(4)

Semi-Finals

Novak Djokovic [1] — 5/7 2/6 6/3 6/2 6/2
Cameron Norrie [9] — 3/6 7/5 2/6 6/3 7/5
Nick Kyrgios — w/o
Rafael Nadal [2] —

Final

Novak Djokovic [1] — 2/6 6/3 6/2 6/4

Novak Djokovic [1] — 4/6 6/3 6/4 7/6(3)

Heavy type denotes seeded players. The figure in brackets against names denotes the order in which they have been seeded. The figure in italics denotes ATP World Tour Ranking – 27.06.22.
(WC)=Wild card. (Q)=Qualifier. (LL)=Lucky loser.

THE GENTLEMEN'S DOUBLES CHAMPIONSHIP 2022
Holders: NIKOLA MEKTIC (CRO) & MATE PAVIC (CRO)

The Champions will become the holders, for the year only, of the CHALLENGE CUPS presented by the OXFORD UNIVERSITY LAWN TENNIS CLUB in 1884 and the late SIR HERBERT WILBERFORCE in 1937. The Champions will each receive a silver three-quarter size replica of the Challenge Cup.
A Silver Salver will be presented to each of the Runners-up, and a Bronze Medal to each defeated semi-finalist. The matches will be the best of five sets. If the score should reach 6-6 in the final set, the match will be decided by a first-to-ten tie-break.

First Round — Second Round — Third Round — Quarter-Finals — Semi-Finals — Final

1. **Rajeev Ram** (USA) & **Joe Salisbury** (GBR) .... [1]
2. Daniel Altmaier (GER) & Carlos Taberner (ESP) ....
   - Rajeev Ram & Joe Salisbury [1] ... 6/3 7/6(5) 7/6(6)
3. Fabrice Martin (FRA) & Hugo Nys (MON) ....
4. Maximo Gonzalez (ARG) & Nathaniel Lammons (USA) .....
   - Fabrice Martin & Hugo Nys ... 5/7 6/7(9) 6/4 7/6(2) 7/5
     - Rajeev Ram & Joe Salisbury [1] ... 6/4 6/4 6/4
5. Aleksandr Nedovyesov (KAZ) & Aisam-Ul-Haq Qureshi (PAK) ...
6. James Duckworth (AUS) & Marcos Giron (USA) ....
   - Aleksandr Nedovyesov & Aisam-Ul-Haq Qureshi ... 6/3 6/7(10) 6/1 6/2
       - Rajeev Ram & Joe Salisbury [1] ... 4/6 6/4 6/3 6/4
(WC) 7. Liam Broady (GBR) & Jay Clarke (GBR) ....
8. **Rafael Matos** (BRA) & **David Vega Hernandez** (ESP) ... [16]
   - Rafael Matos & David Vega Hernandez [16] ... 3/6 7/6(6) 6/4 6/2
     - Rafael Matos & David Vega Hernandez [16] ... 3/6 7/6(6) 5/3 Ret'd
9. **Nicolas Mahut** (FRA) & **Edouard Roger-Vasselin** (FRA).. [12]
10. Francisco Cerundolo (ARG) & Tomas Martin Etcheverry (ARG) ...
    - Nicolas Mahut & Edouard Roger-Vasselin [12] ... 6/1 6/2 6/3
11. Hans Hach Verdugo (MEX) & Philipp Oswald (AUT) ....
12. Roman Jebavy (CZE) & Hunter Reese (USA) ....
    - Hans Hach Verdugo & Philipp Oswald ... 6/2 6/7(6) 4/6 7/6(5) 7/6(9)
      - Nicolas Mahut & Edouard Roger-Vasselin [12] ... 6/7(5) 6/7(4) 7/6(3) 7/6(2) 6/4
13. Maxime Cressy (USA) & Feliciano Lopez (ESP) ....
14. Lukasz Kubot (POL) & Szymon Walkow (POL) ....
    - Lukasz Kubot & Szymon Walkow ... 6/2 7/5 6/3
        - Nicolas Mahut & Edouard Roger-Vasselin [12] ... w/o
15. Steve Johnson (USA) & Sam Querrey (USA) ....
16. **Ivan Dodig** (CRO) & **Austin Krajicek** (USA) .... [8]
    - Ivan Dodig & Austin Krajicek [8] ... 6/3 7/6(2) 6/7(4) 7/5
      - Ivan Dodig & Austin Krajicek [8] ... 7/6(6) 6/3 6/2
17. **Wesley Koolhof** (NED) & **Neal Skupski** (GBR) .... [3]
18. Facundo Bagnis (ARG) & Diego Schwartzman (ARG) ...
    - Wesley Koolhof & Neal Skupski [3] ... 6/3 7/5 6/3
19. Pedro Martinez (ESP) & John-Patrick Smith (AUS) ....
20. Andrey Golubev (KAZ) & Denys Molchanov (UKR) ....
    - Pedro Martinez & John-Patrick Smith ... 6/3 7/6(1) 6/4
      - Wesley Koolhof & Neal Skupski [3] ... 7/6(6) 6/2 7/6(4)
(WC) 21. Alastair Gray (GBR) & Ryan Peniston (GBR) ....
22. Joran Vliegen (BEL) & Jackson Withrow (USA) ....
    - Joran Vliegen & Jackson Withrow ... 6/4 3/6 6/4 6/7(7) 6/4
        - Matthew Ebden & Max Purcell [14] ... 7/5 6/4 3/6 4/6 7/5
23. Andre Goransson (SWE) & Ben McLachlan (JPN) ....
24. **Matthew Ebden** (AUS) & **Max Purcell** (AUS) .... [14]
    - Matthew Ebden & Max Purcell [14] ... 6/7(5) 4/6 6/3 6/4 7/6(8)
      - Matthew Ebden & Max Purcell [14] ... 6/4 6/7(2) 4/6 7/6(3) 6/4
25. **Jamie Murray** (GBR) & **Bruno Soares** (BRA)...........[9]
26. Benjamin Bonzi (FRA) & Arthur Rinderknech (FRA).........
    - Jamie Murray & Bruno Soares [9] ... 6/3 6/4 6/2
27. Sebastian Baez (ARG) & Federico Delbonis (ARG) ....
28. Nikola Cacic (SRB) & Andrea Vavassori (ITA) ....
    - Nikola Cacic & Andrea Vavassori ... 6/2 7/6(6) 7/6(6)
      - Jamie Murray & Bruno Soares [9] ... 6/4 7/6(4) 7/5
29. Joao Sousa (POR) & Jordan Thompson (AUS)............
30. Matwe Middelkoop (NED) & Luke Saville (AUS) ....
    - Joao Sousa & Jordan Thompson ... 2/6 4/6 7/6(4) 6/3 6/3
        - John Peers & Filip Polasek [7] ... 7/6(5) 6/4 4/6 6/4
31. Mackenzie McDonald (USA) & Botic Van De Zandschulp (NED) ...
32. **John Peers** (AUS) & **Filip Polasek** (SVK) .... [7]
    - John Peers & Filip Polasek [7] ... 4/6 4/6 7/5 6/3 6/2
      - John Peers & Filip Polasek [7] ... 7/6(2) 7/5 6/4
33. **Juan Sebastian Cabal** (COL) & **Robert Farah** (COL).... [6]
34. Ugo Humbert (FRA) & Adrian Mannarino (FRA)...........
    - Juan Sebastian Cabal & Robert Farah [6] ... 6/4 6/4 6/4
35. Treat Huey (PHI) & Franko Skugor (CRO) ....
36. Nuno Borges (POR) & Francisco Cabral (POR) ....
    - Nuno Borges & Francisco Cabral ... 7/6(11) 3/6 5/7 6/3 6/2
      - Juan Sebastian Cabal & Robert Farah [6] ... 7/5 6/4 6/2
37. Radu Albot (MDA) & Nikoloz Basilashvili (GEO).........
(A) 38. Sander Arends (NED) & Quentin Halys (FRA).............
    - Radu Albot & Nikoloz Basilashvili ... 7/5 7/6(4) 5/7 1/6 6/4
        - Juan Sebastian Cabal & Robert Farah [6] ... 6/1 6/4 6/4
39. Aljaz Bedene (SLO) & Soonwoo Kwon (KOR) ....
(A) 40. Diego Hidalgo (ECU) & Cristian Rodriguez (COL) ....
    - Diego Hidalgo & Cristian Rodriguez ... 7/6(5) 7/6(4) 6/3
      - Radu Albot & Nikoloz Basilashvili ... 6/4 2/6 3/6 7/6(2) 7/5
41. **Santiago Gonzalez** (MEX) & **Andres Molteni** (ARG)...[13]
(WC) 42. Julian Cash (GBR) & Henry Patten (GBR) ....
    - Santiago Gonzalez & Andres Molteni [13] ... 7/6(5) 6/4 6/2
(A) 43. Robert Galloway (USA) & Max Schnur (USA).................
44. Tallon Griekspoor (NED) & Oscar Otte (GER) ....
    - Robert Galloway & Max Schnur ... 6/1 6/4 6/2
      - Santiago Gonzalez & Andres Molteni [13] ... 7/6(6) 6/4 3/6 6/7(4) 6/4
45. Kamil Majchrzak (POL) & Jan Zielinski (POL)............
46. Laslo Djere (SRB) & Dusan Lajovic (SRB)...............
    - Kamil Majchrzak & Jan Zielinski ... 5/7 5/7 7/5 6/3 6/4
        - Denis Kudla & Jack Sock ... 6/4 6/2 6/4
47. Denis Kudla (USA) & Jack Sock (USA).................
48. **Marcelo Arevalo** (ESA) & **Jean-Julien Rojer** (NED) .... [4]
    - Denis Kudla & Jack Sock ... 7/6(4) 6/3 6/4
      - Denis Kudla & Jack Sock ... 4/6 3/1 Ret'd
49. **Tim Puetz** (GER) & **Michael Venus** (NZL) ....[5]
50. Raven Klaasen (RSA) & Marcelo Melo (BRA)...........
    - Raven Klaasen & Marcelo Melo ... 4/6 7/6(2) 7/5 1/6 7/6(6)
51. Julio Peralta (CHI) & Alejandro Tabilo (CHI)...............
(WC) 52. Jonny O'Mara (GBR) & Ken Skupski (GBR) ....
    - Jonny O'Mara & Ken Skupski ... 6/2 6/3 6/4
      - Jonny O'Mara & Ken Skupski ... 6/2 6/4 6/4
53. Ariel Behar (URU) & Gonzalo Escobar (ECU)..............
(WC) 54. Arthur Fery (GBR) & Felix Gill (GBR) ....
    - Arthur Fery & Felix Gill ... 7/5 7/6(8) 7/6(3)
        - Kevin Krawietz & Andreas Mies [11] ... 7/6(6) 6/4 6/4
55. Sadio Doumbia (FRA) & Fabien Reboul (FRA)...........
56. **Kevin Krawietz** (GER) & **Andreas Mies** (GER) .... [11]
    - Kevin Krawietz & Andreas Mies [11] ... 5/7 6/4 7/6(3) 6/1
      - Kevin Krawietz & Andreas Mies [11] ... 7/6(5) 6/3 6/4
57. **Lloyd Glasspool** (GBR) & **Harri Heliovaara** (FIN) ... [15]
58. Hugo Gaston (FRA) & Lorenzo Musetti (ITA).............
    - Lloyd Glasspool & Harri Heliovaara [15] ... 6/3 6/3 6/4
59. William Blumberg (USA) & Casper Ruud (NOR)...........
60. Nicolas Barrientos (COL) & Miguel Angel Reyes-Varela (MEX) ...
    - William Blumberg & Casper Ruud ... 4/6 6/3 6/7(5) 2/6 7/6(7)
      - Lloyd Glasspool & Harri Heliovaara [15] ... 6/1 3/6 6/3 3/6 6/4
61. Tomislav Brkic (BIH) & Ramkumar Ramanathan (IND) ...
(A) 62. Nicholas Monroe (USA) & Tommy Paul (USA) ....
    - Nicholas Monroe & Tommy Paul ... 6/3 7/6(5) 7/6(5)
        - Nikola Mektic & Mate Pavic [2] ... 6/2 3/6 6/3 6/2
63. Benoit Paire (FRA) & Albert Ramos-Vinolas (ESP) ....
64. **Nikola Mektic** (CRO) & **Mate Pavic** (CRO) ....[2]
    - Nikola Mektic & Mate Pavic [2] ... 6/4 6/1 6/1
      - Nikola Mektic & Mate Pavic [2] ... 6/2 3/6 6/3 6/2

Quarter-Finals / Semi-Finals / Final:

- Rajeev Ram & Joe Salisbury [1] ... 6/3 6/7(T) 7/6(9) 6/4 6/2
- Nicolas Mahut & Edouard Roger-Vasselin [12]
  - Matthew Ebden & Max Purcell [14] ... 6/4 6/4 6/2
- Matthew Ebden & Max Purcell [14]
- John Peers & Filip Polasek [7]
    - Matthew Ebden & Max Purcell [14] ... 3/6 6/7(T) 7/6(9) 6/4 6/2
- Juan Sebastian Cabal & Robert Farah [6] ... 6/3 6/3 6/7(3) 1/1 Ret'd
- Denis Kudla & Jack Sock
  - Nikola Mektic & Mate Pavic [2] ... 6/7(2) 7/6(0) 4/6 6/2 7/6(4)
- Kevin Krawietz & Andreas Mies [11]
- Nikola Mektic & Mate Pavic [2] ... 6/4 6/3 6/3

Final:
Matthew Ebden & Max Purcell [14] ... 7/6(5) 6/7(3) 4/6 6/4 7/6(2)

Heavy type denotes seeded players. The figure in brackets against names denotes the order in which they have been seeded.
(WC)=Wild cards. (Q)=Qualifiers. (LL)=Lucky losers.

THE LADIES' SINGLES CHAMPIONSHIP 2022
Holder: ASHLEIGH BARTY (AUS)

The Champion will become the holder, for the year only, of the CHALLENGE TROPHY presented by The All England Lawn Tennis and Croquet Club in 1886. The Champion will receive a silver three-quarter size replica of the Challenge Trophy.
A Silver Salver will be presented to the Runner-up and a Bronze Medal to each defeated semi-finalist. The matches will be the best of three sets. If the score should reach 6-6 in the final set, the match will be decided by a first-to-ten tie-break.

First Round	Second Round	Third Round	Fourth Round	Quarter-Finals	Semi-Finals	Final
1. Iga Swiatek [1] (1) (POL)	Iga Swiatek [1] — 6/0 6/3					
(Q) 2. Jana Fett (267) (CRO)		Iga Swiatek [1]				
(WC) 3. Sonay Kartal (270) (GBR)	Lesley Pattinama Kerkhove — 6/4 3/6 6/1					
(LL) 4. Lesley Pattinama Kerkhove (135) (NED)			Alize Cornet			
5. Claire Liu (74) (USA)	Claire Liu — 7/5 6/3		6/4 6/2			
6. Nuria Parrizas Diaz (51) (ESP)		Alize Cornet				
7. Alize Cornet (33) (FRA)	Alize Cornet — 6/3 7/6(5)	6/3 6/3				
8. Yulia Putintseva [27] (32) (KAZ)				Ajla Tomljanovic		
9. Jil Teichmann [18] (22) (SUI)	Ajla Tomljanovic — 6/2 6/3			4/6 6/4 6/3		
10. Ajla Tomljanovic (45) (AUS)		Ajla Tomljanovic				
(Q) 11. Catherine Harrison (259) (USA)	Catherine Harrison — 6/1 6/4	6/2 6/2				
12. Arantxa Rus (77) (NED)			Ajla Tomljanovic			
13. Viktorija Golubic (55) (SUI)	Viktorija Golubic — 6/4 6/3		2/6 6/4 6/3			
14. Andrea Petkovic (57) (GER)		Barbora Krejcikova [13]				
15. Maryna Zanevska (66) (BEL)	Barbora Krejcikova [13] — 7/6(4) 6/3	6/3 6/4				
16. Barbora Krejcikova [13] (14) (CZE)					Elena Rybakina [17]	
17. Garbine Muguruza [9] (10) (ESP)	Greet Minnen — 6/4 6/0				4/6 6/2 6/3	
18. Greet Minnen (88) (BEL)		Qinwen Zheng				
19. Qinwen Zheng (54) (CHN)	Qinwen Zheng — 7/6(1) 7/5	6/4 6/1				
20. Sloane Stephens (47) (USA)			Elena Rybakina [17]			
(Q) 21. Emina Bektas (200) (USA)	Bianca Andreescu — 6/1 6/3		7/6(4) 7/5			
22. Bianca Andreescu (70) (CAN)		Elena Rybakina [17]				
(LL) 23. Coco Vandeweghe (122) (USA)	Elena Rybakina [17] — 7/6(2) 7/5	6/4 7/6(5)				
24. Elena Rybakina [17] (21) (KAZ)				Elena Rybakina [17]		
25. Shelby Rogers [30] (42) (USA)	Petra Martic — 6/2 7/6(5)			7/5 6/3		
26. Petra Martic (73) (CRO)		Petra Martic				
27. Kristina Kucova (89) (SVK)	Kristina Kucova — 7/5 6/0	7/6(4) 6/3				
28. Laura Pigossi (124) (BRA)			Petra Martic			
29. Rebeka Masarova (140) (ESP)	Harriet Dart — . 6/4		6/2 7/6(5)			
30. Harriet Dart (114) (GBR)		Jessica Pegula [8]				
31. Donna Vekic (90) (CRO)	Jessica Pegula [8] — 6/3 7/6(2)	4/6 6/3 6/1				
32. Jessica Pegula [8] (8) (USA)						Elena Rybakina [17]
33. Paula Badosa [4] (3) (ESP)	Paula Badosa [4] — 6/2 6/1					6/3 6/3
(Q) 34. Louisa Chirico (218) (USA)		Paula Badosa [4]				
35. Irina Bara (115) (ROU)	Irina Bara — 6/2 6/4	6/3 6/2				
36. Chloe Paquet (101) (FRA)			Paula Badosa [4]			
37. Ana Bogdan (108) (ROU)	Ana Bogdan — 6/2 6/2		7/5 7/6(4)			
38. Dayana Yastremska (80) (UKR)		Petra Kvitova [25]				
39. Jasmine Paolini (62) (ITA)	Petra Kvitova [25] — 2/6 6/4 6/2	6/1 7/6(5)				
40. Petra Kvitova [25] (31) (CZE)				Simona Halep [16]		
41. Camila Giorgi [21] (26) (ITA)	Magdalena Frech — 7/6(4) 6/1			6/1 6/2		
42. Magdalena Frech (92) (POL)		Magdalena Frech				
43. Rebecca Peterson (95) (SWE)	Anna Karolina Schmiedlova — 7/5 0/6 6/3	6/4 6/4				
44. Anna Karolina Schmiedlova (84) (SVK)			Simona Halep [16]			
45. Kirsten Flipkens (97) (BEL)	Kirsten Flipkens — 7/5 6/2		6/4 6/1			
(Q) 46. Jaimee Fourlis (177) (AUS)		Simona Halep [16]				
47. Karolina Muchova (81) (CZE)	Simona Halep [16] — 6/3 6/2	7/5 6/4				
48. Simona Halep [16] (20) (ROU)					Simona Halep [16]	
49. Coco Gauff [11] (13) (USA)	Coco Gauff [11] — 2/6 6/3 7/5				6/2 6/4	
50. Elena-Gabriela Ruse (53) (ROU)		Coco Gauff [11]				
51. Mihaela Buzarnescu (126) (ROU)	Mihaela Buzarnescu — 6/4 6/2	6/2 6/3				
(Q) 52. Nastasja Schunk (161) (GER)			Amanda Anisimova [20]			
53. Madison Brengle (56) (USA)	Lauren Davis — 6/2 7/5		6/7(4) 6/2 6/1			
54. Lauren Davis (93) (USA)		Amanda Anisimova [20]				
(LL) 55. Yue Yuan (151) (CHN)	Amanda Anisimova [20] — 6/3 6/4	2/6 6/3 6/4				
56. Amanda Anisimova [20] (25) (USA)				Amanda Anisimova [20]		
57. Sara Sorribes Tormo [32] (39) (ESP)	Sara Sorribes Tormo [32] — 6/2 6/1			6/2 6/3		
(Q) 58. Christina McHale (239) (USA)		Harmony Tan				
(WC) 59. Serena Williams (1223) (USA)	Harmony Tan — 7/5 1/6 7/6(7)	6/3 6/4				
60. Harmony Tan (121) (FRA)			Harmony Tan			
61. Clara Burel (94) (FRA)	Katie Boulter — 6/3 6/3		6/1 6/1			
(WC) 62. Katie Boulter (136) (GBR)		Katie Boulter				
63. Tereza Martincova (60) (CZE)	Karolina Pliskova [6] — 7/6(1) 7/5	3/6 7/6(4) 6/4				
64. Karolina Pliskova [6] (7) (CZE)				Marie Bouzkova		
65. Danielle Collins [7] (9) (USA)	Marie Bouzkova — 5/7 6/4 6/3			6/2 6/3		
66. Marie Bouzkova (64) (CZE)		Marie Bouzkova				
67. Lucia Bronzetti (72) (ITA)	Ann Li — 6/1 6/4	6/0 6/3				
68. Ann Li (68) (USA)			Marie Bouzkova			
69. Katerina Siniakova (65) (CZE)	Maja Chwalinska — 6/0 7/5		6/2 6/3			
(Q) 70. Maja Chwalinska (185) (POL)		Alison Riske-Amritraj [28]				
71. Ylena In-Albon (170) (SUI)	Alison Riske-Amritraj [28] — 6/2 6/4	3/6 6/1 6/0				
72. Alison Riske-Amritraj [28] (40) (USA)					Marie Bouzkova	
73. Shuai Zhang [33] (41) (CHN)	Shuai Zhang [33] — 6/4 6/0				7/5 6/2	
74. Misaki Doi (100) (JPN)		Shuai Zhang [33]				
75. Marta Kostyuk (79) (UKR)	Marta Kostyuk — 4/6 6/4 6/4	7/6(6) 6/2				
(WC) 76. Katie Swan (216) (GBR)			Caroline Garcia			
77. Caroline Garcia (75) (FRA)	Caroline Garcia — 4/6 6/1 7/6(4)		7/6(3) 7/6(5)			
(WC) 78. Yuriko Miyazaki (234) (GBR)		Caroline Garcia				
79. Alison Van Uytvanck (46) (BEL)	Emma Raducanu [10] — 6/3 6/3	6/3 6/3				
80. Emma Raducanu [10] (11) (GBR)				Ons Jabeur [3]		
81. Angelique Kerber [15] (18) (GER)	Angelique Kerber [15] — 6/0 7/5			3/6 6/1 6/1		
82. Kristina Mladenovic (119) (FRA)		Angelique Kerber [15]				
83. Magda Linette (67) (POL)	Magda Linette — 6/1 6/4	6/3 6/4				
(Q) 84. Fernanda Contreras Gomez (162) (MEX)			Elise Mertens [24]			
85. Tamara Zidansek (59) (SLO)	Panna Udvardy — 6/4 7/6(1)		6/4 7/5			
86. Panna Udvardy (98) (HUN)		Elise Mertens [24]				
87. Camila Osorio (61) (COL)	Elise Mertens [24] — 1/6 6/2 4/2 Ret'd	3/6 7/6(5) 7/5				
88. Elise Mertens [24] (29) (BEL)					Ons Jabeur [3]	
89. Kaia Kanepi [31] (38) (EST)	Diane Parry — 6/4 6/4				7/6(9) 6/4	
90. Diane Parry (82) (FRA)		Diane Parry				
91. Clara Tauson (52) (DEN)	Mai Hontama — 4/1 Ret'd	6/3 6/2				
(Q) 92. Mai Hontama (133) (JPN)			Ons Jabeur [3]			
93. Rebecca Marino (109) (CAN)	Katarzyna Kawa — 6/4 3/6 7/5		6/2 6/3			
(Q) 94. Katarzyna Kawa (129) (POL)		Ons Jabeur [3]				
(Q) 95. Mirjam Bjorklund (134) (SWE)	Ons Jabeur [3] — 6/1 6/1	6/4 6/0				
96. Ons Jabeur [3] (4) (TUN)				Ons Jabeur [3]		
97. Maria Sakkari [5] (5) (GRE)	Maria Sakkari [5] — 6/1 6/4			6/2 3/6 6/1		
(Q) 98. Zoe Hives (596) (AUS)		Maria Sakkari [5]				
(WC) 99. Daria Saville (104) (AUS)	Viktoriya Tomova — 7/5 3/6 7/5	6/1 6/4				
100. Viktoriya Tomova (131) (BUL)			Tatjana Maria			
(Q) 101. Astra Sharma (143) (AUS)	Tatjana Maria — 4/6 6/3 6/4		6/3 7/5			
102. Tatjana Maria (106) (GER)		Tatjana Maria				
103. Aleksandra Krunic (103) (SRB)	Sorana Cirstea [26] — 7/6(5) 7/6(1)	6/3 1/6 7/5				
104. Sorana Cirstea [26] (34) (ROU)				Tatjana Maria		
105. Martina Trevisan [22] (27) (ITA)	Elisabetta Cocciaretto — 6/2 6/0			5/7 7/5 7/5		
106. Elisabetta Cocciaretto (113) (ITA)		Irina-Camelia Begu				
107. Ekaterine Gorgodze (112) (GEO)	Irina-Camelia Begu — 6/4 6/1	6/4 6/4				
108. Irina-Camelia Begu (44) (ROU)			Jelena Ostapenko [12]			
(Q) 109. Yanina Wickmayer (749) (BEL)	Yanina Wickmayer — 6/4 6/2		3/6 6/1 6/1			
110. Lin Zhu (96) (CHN)		Jelena Ostapenko [12]				
111. Oceane Dodin (85) (FRA)	Jelena Ostapenko [12] — 6/4 6/2	6/2 6/2				
112. Jelena Ostapenko [12] (16) (LAT)					Tatjana Maria	
113. Belinda Bencic [14] (17) (SUI)	Qiang Wang — 6/4 5/7 6/2				4/6 6/2 7/5	
114. Qiang Wang (146) (CHN)		Heather Watson				
115. Tamara Korpatsch (105) (GER)	Heather Watson — 6/7(7) 7/5 6/2	7/5 6/4				
116. Heather Watson (102) (GBR)			Heather Watson			
(Q) 117. Maddison Inglis (127) (AUS)	Dalma Galfi — 5/7 6/3 6/4		7/6(6) 6/2			
118. Dalma Galfi (99) (HUN)		Kaja Juvan				
119. Kaja Juvan (58) (SLO)	Kaja Juvan — 6/4 4/6 6/2	7/5 6/3				
120. Beatriz Haddad Maia [23] (48) (BRA)				Jule Niemeier		
121. Anhelina Kalinina [29] (35) (UKR)	Anhelina Kalinina [29] — 4/6 6/2 6/4			6/2 6/4		
122. Anna Bondar (63) (HUN)		Lesia Tsurenko				
(WC) 123. Jodie Burrage (235) (GBR)	Lesia Tsurenko — 6/2 6/3	3/6 6/4 6/3				
124. Lesia Tsurenko (116) (UKR)			Jule Niemeier			
125. Jule Niemeier (97) (GER)	Jule Niemeier — 6/1 6/4		6/4 3/6 6/3			
126. Xiyu Wang (111) (CHN)		Jule Niemeier				
127. Bernarda Pera (118) (USA)	Anett Kontaveit [2] — 7/5 6/1	6/4 6/0				
128. Anett Kontaveit [2] (2) (EST)						

Heavy type denotes seeded players. The figure in brackets against names denotes the order in which they have been seeded. The figure in italics denotes WTA Ranking – 27.06.22.
(WC)=Wild card. (Q)=Qualifier. (LL)=Lucky loser.

THE LADIES' DOUBLES CHAMPIONSHIP 2022
Holders: SU-WEI HSIEH (TPE) & ELISE MERTENS (BEL)

The Champions will become the holders, for the year only, of the CHALLENGE CUPS presented by H.R.H. PRINCESS MARINA, DUCHESS OF KENT, the late President of The All England Lawn Tennis and Croquet Club in 1949 and The All England Lawn Tennis and Croquet Club in 2001. The Champions will each receive a silver three-quarter size replica of the Challenge Cup. A Silver Salver will be presented to each of the Runners-up and a Bronze Medal to each defeated semi-finalist. The matches will be the best of three sets. If the score should reach 6-6 in the final set, the match will be decided by a first-to-ten tie-break.

First Round	Second Round	Third Round	Quarter-Finals	Semi-Finals	Final

1. **Elise Mertens** (BEL) & **Shuai Zhang** (CHN)...............[1]
2. Anna Bondar (HUN) & Greet Minnen (BEL) ....
   - **Elise Mertens** & **Shuai Zhang** [1] — 6/3 6/1
3. Viktorija Golubic (SUI) & Camila Osorio (COL)................
(WC) 4. Sonay Kartal (GBR) & Nell Miller (GBR) ....
   - Viktorija Golubic & Camila Osorio — 7/5 6/4
   - Elise Mertens & Shuai Zhang [1] — 6/3 6/2
5. Kaia Kanepi (EST) & Renata Voracova (CZE) ....
(WC) 6. Alicia Barnett (GBR) & Olivia Nicholls (GBR)................
   - Alicia Barnett & Olivia Nicholls — 6/1 4/6 6/2
7. Valentini Grammatikopoulou (GRE) & Peangtarn Plipuech (THA) ...
(A) 8. **Nadiia Kichenok** (UKR) & **Raluca Olaru** (ROU).......[15]
   - **Nadiia Kichenok** & **Raluca Olaru** [15] — 6/2 6/3
   - Nadiia Kichenok & Raluca Olaru [15] — 3/6 6/4 7/6(5)
   - Elise Mertens & Shuai Zhang [1] — 6/4 6/3
9. **Yifan Xu** (CHN) & **Zhaoxuan Yang** (CHN)................[9]
10. Lucia Bronzetti (ITA) & Julia Lohoff (GER) ....
   - **Yifan Xu** & **Zhaoxuan Yang** [9] — 6/3 6/4
11. Jule Niemeier (GER) & Andrea Petkovic (GER) ....
12. Miyu Kato (JPN) & Aldila Sutjiadi (INA) ....
   - Jule Niemeier & Andrea Petkovic — 7/6(3) 5/7 7/6(12)
   - Yifan Xu & Zhaoxuan Yang [9] — 6/3 0/6 7/5
13. Alize Cornet (FRA) & Diane Parry (FRA) ....
14. Magda Linette (POL) & Bernarda Pera (USA) ....
   - Alize Cornet & Diane Parry — 6/1 6/7(6) 6/4
   - Alexa Guarachi & Andreja Klepac [7] — 6/3 7/5
15. Monique Adamczak (AUS) & Katarzyna Kawa (POL)...
16. **Alexa Guarachi** (CHI) & **Andreja Klepac** (SLO).......[7]
   - **Alexa Guarachi** & **Andreja Klepac** [7] — 6/3 6/4
   - Alexa Guarachi & Andreja Klepac [7] — 6/3 6/2
   - Elise Mertens & Shuai Zhang [1] — 6/3 6/2
17. **Gabriela Dabrowski** (CAN) & **Giuliana Olmos** (MEX)...[3]
18. Yulia Putintseva (KAZ) & Yanina Wickmayer (BEL).........
   - **Gabriela Dabrowski** & **Giuliana Olmos** [3] — 6/7(2) 6/3 6/2
19. Marta Kostyuk (UKR) & Tereza Martincova (CZE)............
20. Madison Brengle (USA) & Lauren Davis (USA) ....
   - Marta Kostyuk & Tereza Martincova — 6/3 6/4
   - Gabriela Dabrowski & Giuliana Olmos [3] — 7/5 3/6 6/3
21. Irina Bara (ROU) & Ekaterine Gorgodze (GEO) ....
22. Danielle Collins (USA) & Desirae Krawczyk (USA) ....
   - Danielle Collins & Desirae Krawczyk — 6/3 6/2
   - Danielle Collins & Desirae Krawczyk — 6/1 6/3
23. Oksana Kalashnikova (GEO) & Katarzyna Piter (POL) .
24. **Marie Bouzkova** (CZE) & **Tereza Mihalikova** (SVK)...[16]
   - **Marie Bouzkova** & **Tereza Mihalikova** [16] — 3/6 7/6(5) 6/4
   - Danielle Collins & Desirae Krawczyk — 6/4 6/3
25. **Alicja Rosolska** (POL) & **Erin Routliffe** (NZL)...........[11]
26. Irina-Camelia Begu (ROU) & Anhelina Kalinina (UKR) ...
   - **Alicja Rosolska** & **Erin Routliffe** [11] — 6/4 6/4
27. Catherine Harrison (USA) & Sabrina Santamaria (USA) ...
28. Kaja Juvan (SLO) & Tamara Zidansek (SLO) ....
   - Catherine Harrison & Sabrina Santamaria — 2/6 6/4 5/2 Ret'd
   - Alicja Rosolska & Erin Routliffe [11] — 6/7(3) 7/5 7/6(7)
   - Danielle Collins & Desirae Krawczyk — 6/1 6/7(4) 6/3
29. Clara Burel (FRA) & Chloe Paquet (FRA).....................
(A) 30. Xinyun Han (CHN) & Lin Zhu (CHN) ....
   - Xinyun Han & Lin Zhu — 6/3 7/6(5)
   - Asia Muhammad & Ena Shibahara [5] — 6/1 6/4
(WC) 31. Sarah Beth Grey (GBR) & Yuriko Miyazaki (GBR) ....
32. **Asia Muhammad** (USA) & **Ena Shibahara** (JPN).......[5]
   - **Asia Muhammad** & **Ena Shibahara** [5] — 6/1 6/1
   - Alicja Rosolska & Erin Routliffe [11] — 6/4 7/6(3)
33. **Shuko Aoyama** (JPN) & **Hao-Ching Chan** (TPE) ......[8]
34. Xiyu Wang (CHN) & Qinwen Zheng (CHN) ....
   - **Shuko Aoyama** & **Hao-Ching Chan** [8] — 7/5 6/3
35. Jasmine Paolini (ITA) & Martina Trevisan (ITA) ....
(WC) 36. Naiktha Bains (GBR) & Maia Lumsden (GBR) ....
   - Naiktha Bains & Maia Lumsden — 6/1 7/5
   - Shuko Aoyama & Hao-Ching Chan [8] — 6/1 6/4
37. Ulrikke Eikeri (NOR) & Astra Sharma (AUS)................
38. Alison Riske-Amritraj (USA) & Coco Vandeweghe (USA)...
   - Alison Riske-Amritraj & Coco Vandeweghe — 0/6 6/4 6/4
   - Shuko Aoyama & Hao-Ching Chan [8] — 6/4 4/6 7/6(3)
39. Aliona Bolsova (ESP) & Ingrid Neel (USA)..................
40. **Latisha Chan** (TPE) & **Samantha Stosur** (AUS).........[12]
   - Aliona Bolsova & Ingrid Neel — 7/6(4) 6/1
   - Alison Riske-Amritraj & Coco Vandeweghe — 7/6(1) 6/3
41. **Natela Dzalamidze** (GEO) & **Aleksandra Krunic** (SRB)...[13]
(A) 42. Anna-Lena Friedsam (GER) & Ann Li (USA) ....
   - **Natela Dzalamidze** & **Aleksandra Krunic** [13] — 6/3 7/5
43. Emina Bektas (USA) & Kristina Kucova (SVK).............
(WC) 44. Harriet Dart (GBR) & Heather Watson (GBR) ....
   - Harriet Dart & Heather Watson — 6/2 6/4
   - Harriet Dart & Heather Watson — 6/4 6/2
(WC) 45. Jodie Burrage (GBR) & Eden Silva (GBR) ....
46. Arianne Hartono (NED) & Demi Schuurs (NED) ....
   - Arianne Hartono & Demi Schuurs — 6/3 6/4
   - Lyudmyla Kichenok & Jelena Ostapenko [4] — 6/2 7/6(5)
47. Oceane Dodin (FRA) & Tatjana Maria (GER)..............
48. **Lyudmyla Kichenok** (UKR) & **Jelena Ostapenko** (LAT)...[4]
   - **Lyudmyla Kichenok** & **Jelena Ostapenko** [4] — 2/6 7/5 6/3
   - Lyudmyla Kichenok & Jelena Ostapenko [4] — 5/7 6/4 6/2
   - Lyudmyla Kichenok & Jelena Ostapenko [4] — 4/6 6/1 7/5
49. **Lucie Hradecka** (CZE) & **Sania Mirza** (IND)...............[6]
50. Magdalena Frech (POL) & Beatriz Haddad Maia (BRA) ...
   - Magdalena Frech & Beatriz Haddad Maia — 4/6 6/4 6/2
51. Daria Saville (AUS) & Ajla Tomljanovic (AUS) ....
52. Viktoria Kuzmova (SVK) & Arantxa Rus (NED) ....
   - Viktoria Kuzmova & Arantxa Rus — 6/3 6/3
   - Magdalena Frech & Beatriz Haddad Maia — 6/4 5/7 6/3
(A) 53. Elisabetta Cocciaretto (ITA) & Viktoriya Tomova (BUL)...
54. Maryna Zanevska (BEL) & Kimberley Zimmermann (BEL)...
   - Elisabetta Cocciaretto & Viktoriya Tomova — 6/3 7/6(2)
   - Nicole Melichar-Martinez & Ellen Perez [10] — 6/4 6/4
55. Kaitlyn Christian (USA) & Panna Udvardy (HUN)..........
56. **Nicole Melichar-Martinez** (USA) & **Ellen Perez** (AUS)...[10]
   - **Nicole Melichar-Martinez** & **Ellen Perez** [10] — 6/3 7/5
   - Nicole Melichar-Martinez & Ellen Perez [10] — 6/1 6/1
57. **Monica Niculescu** (ROU) & **Elena-Gabriela Ruse** (ROU)...[14]
58. Kirsten Flipkens (BEL) & Sara Sorribes Tormo (ESP) ...
   - Kirsten Flipkens & Sara Sorribes Tormo — 7/6(3) 6/2
59. Dalma Galfi (HUN) & Dayana Yastremska (UKR)...........
60. Belinda Bencic (SUI) & Storm Sanders (AUS) ....
   - Belinda Bencic & Storm Sanders — 6/2 6/7(7) 7/6(16)
   - Kirsten Flipkens & Sara Sorribes Tormo — 3/6 6/3 6/2
61. Anett Kontaveit (EST) & Shelby Rogers (USA)...............
62. Vivian Heisen (GER) & Samantha Murray Sharan (GBR)...
   - Anett Kontaveit & Shelby Rogers — 6/2 6/4
   - Barbora Krejcikova & Katerina Siniakova [2] — 7/6(8) 6/3
63. Elixane Lechemia (FRA) & Nuria Parrizas Diaz (ESP) ...
64. **Barbora Krejcikova** (CZE) & **Katerina Siniakova** (CZE)....[2]
   - **Barbora Krejcikova** & **Katerina Siniakova** [2] — 6/1 6/1

Quarter-Finals:
- Elise Mertens & Shuai Zhang [1] — 6/3 6/2
- Danielle Collins & Desirae Krawczyk — 6/4 7/6(3)
- Lyudmyla Kichenok & Jelena Ostapenko [4] — 6/1 6/1
- Barbora Krejcikova & Katerina Siniakova [2] — 7/6(2) 6/2

Semi-Finals:
- Elise Mertens & Shuai Zhang [1] — 6/2 3/6 6/3
- Barbora Krejcikova & Katerina Siniakova [2] — 1/6 7/6(2) 6/2

Final:
- **Barbora Krejcikova & Katerina Siniakova [2]** — 6/2 6/4

Heavy type denotes seeded players. The figure in brackets against names denotes the order in which they have been seeded.
(WC)=Wild cards. (Q)=Qualifiers. (LL)=Lucky losers.

THE MIXED DOUBLES CHAMPIONSHIP 2022
Holders: NEAL SKUPSKI (GBR) & DESIRAE KRAWCZYK (USA)

The Champions will become the holders, for the year only, of the CHALLENGE CUPS presented by members of the family of the late Mr. S. H. SMITH in 1949 and The All England Lawn Tennis and Croquet Club in 2001. The Champions will each receive a silver three-quarter size replica of the Challenge Cup. A Silver Salver will be presented to each of the Runners-up and a Bronze Medal to each defeated semi-finalist. The matches will be the best of three sets. If the score should reach 6-6 in the final set, the match will be decided by a first-to-ten tie-break.

First Round	Second Round	Quarter-Finals	Semi-Finals	Final
1. Jean-Julien Rojer (NED) & Ena Shibahara (JPN) ...... [1]	Jean-Julien Rojer & Ena Shibahara [1]			
2. Austin Krajicek (USA) & Alexa Guarachi (CHI)	6/4 7/6(10)	Matthew Ebden & Samantha Stosur		
3. Matthew Ebden (AUS) & Samantha Stosur (AUS)........	Matthew Ebden & Samantha Stosur	6/3 6/7(5) 6/4		
(A) 4. Joran Vliegen (BEL) & Ulrikke Eikeri (NOR)................	4/6 7/6(6) 6/4		Matthew Ebden & Samantha Stosur	
5. Michael Venus (NZL) & Alicja Rosolska (POL)	Jamie Murray & Venus Williams		6/3 6/1	
(WC) 6. Jamie Murray (GBR) & Venus Williams (USA)	6/3 6/7(3) 6/3	Jonny O'Mara & Alicia Barnett		
(WC) 7. Jonny O'Mara (GBR) & Alicia Barnett (GBR)	Jonny O'Mara & Alicia Barnett	3/6 6/4 7/6(16)		
8. Marcelo Arevalo (ESA) & Giuliana Olmos (MEX)..... [5]	6/2 3/6 7/5			
9. Nicolas Mahut (FRA) & Shuai Zhang (CHN) .... [3]	Nicolas Mahut & Shuai Zhang [3]			
10. Gonzalo Escobar (ECU) & Lucie Hradecka (CZE)........	6/3 6/4	Jack Sock & Coco Gauff		
11. Jack Sock (USA) & Coco Gauff (USA)........................	Jack Sock & Coco Gauff	6/4 7/6(3)		
(WC) 12. Kyle Edmund (GBR) & Olivia Nicholls (GBR)............	6/4 6/1		Jack Sock & Coco Gauff	
13. Maximo Gonzalez (ARG) & Kaitlyn Christian (USA)......	Edouard Roger-Vasselin & Alize Cornet		6/3 6/4	
14. Edouard Roger-Vasselin (FRA) & Alize Cornet (FRA) .	6/7(6) 7/6(8) 6/4	Edouard Roger-Vasselin & Alize Cornet		
15. Max Purcell (AUS) & Storm Sanders (AUS)	Filip Polasek & Andreja Klepac [8]	7/5 6/2		
16. Filip Polasek (SVK) & Andreja Klepac (SLO)............ [8]	7/6(2) 4/6 6/3			Matthew Ebden & Samantha Stosur 6/3 5/7 7/5
17. Mate Pavic (CRO) & Sania Mirza (IND) .... [6]	Mate Pavic & Sania Mirza [6]			
18. David Vega Hernandez (ESP) & Natela Dzalamidze (GEO)...	6/4 3/6 7/6(3)	Mate Pavic & Sania Mirza [6]		
(WC) 19. Ivan Dodig (CRO) & Latisha Chan (TPE)	Ivan Dodig & Latisha Chan	w/o		
20. Andreas Mies (GER) & Erin Routliffe (NZL)................	6/2 5/7 6/4		Mate Pavic & Sania Mirza [6]	
21. Rafael Matos (BRA) & Lyudmyla Kichenok (UKR)........	Bruno Soares & Beatriz Haddad Maia		6/4 3/6 7/5	
22. Bruno Soares (BRA) & Beatriz Haddad Maia (BRA)	7/6(6) 6/3	John Peers & Gabriela Dabrowski [4]		
23. Ariel Behar (URU) & Demi Schuurs (NED)	John Peers & Gabriela Dabrowski [4]	4/6 6/3 6/0		
24. John Peers (AUS) & Gabriela Dabrowski (CAN).... [4]	6/3 6/4			Neal Skupski & Desirae Krawczyk [2] 6/4 6/3
25. Robert Farah (COL) & Jelena Ostapenko (LAT) ...... [7]	Robert Farah & Jelena Ostapenko [7]			
26. Ben McLachlan (JPN) & Hao-Ching Chan (TPE)	7/5 3/6 6/1	Robert Farah & Jelena Ostapenko [7]		
(A) 27. Nikola Cacic (SRB) & Aleksandra Krunic (SRB)	Nikola Cacic & Aleksandra Krunic	7/6(5) 6/4		
28. Kevin Krawietz (GER) & Nicole Melichar-Martinez (USA)....	3/6 6/3 6/3		Neal Skupski & Desirae Krawczyk [2]	
29. Matwe Middelkoop (NED) & Ellen Perez (AUS)	Matwe Middelkoop & Ellen Perez		7/6(6) 6/1	
30. Santiago Gonzalez (MEX) & Zhaoxuan Yang (CHN)	6/2 7/5	Neal Skupski & Desirae Krawczyk [2]		
31. Thanasi Kokkinakis (AUS) & Asia Muhammad (USA) ...	Neal Skupski & Desirae Krawczyk [2]	7/5 6/2		
32. Neal Skupski (GBR) & Desirae Krawczyk (USA) ...... [2]	7/5 6/7(4) 6/4			

Neal Skupski & Desirae Krawczyk [2]

Matthew Ebden & Samantha Stosur

Neal Skupski & Desirae Krawczyk [2] 4/6 7/5 6/4

Heavy type denotes seeded players. The figure in brackets against names denotes the order in which they have been seeded.
(A)=Alternates. (WC)=Wild cards.

The sun sets behind the Millennium Building as eventual champions Neal Skupski and Desirae Krawczyk take on Mate Pavic and Sania Mirza in their mixed doubles semi-final on No.2 Court

THE GENTLEMEN'S WHEELCHAIR SINGLES 2022
Holder: JOACHIM GERARD (BEL)

The Champion will become the holder, for the year only, of a Cup presented by The All England Lawn Tennis and Croquet Club. The Champion will receive a three-quarter size replica of the Cup. A Silver Salver will be presented to the Runner-up.
The matches will be the best of three tie-break sets.

First Round   Semi-final   Final

1. **Shingo Kunieda [1]** *(1)* .... (JPN)
    Shingo Kunieda [1] .... 6/1 6/7(5) 6/1

2. Tom Egberink *(6)* .... (NED)
    Shingo Kunieda [1] 6/2 6/1

3. Joachim Gerard *(7)* .... (BEL)
    Joachim Gerard .... 6/4 7/6(2)

(WC) 4. Tokito Oda *(8)* .... (JPN)

5. Gustavo Fernandez *(3)* .... (ARG)
    Gustavo Fernandez 6/4 6/1

6. Nicolas Peifer *(9)* .... (FRA)
    Alfie Hewett [2] .... 2/6 7/6(3) 6/4

7. Gordon Reid *(4)* .... (GBR)
    Alfie Hewett [2] 6/2 3/6 6/4

8. **Alfie Hewett [2]** *(2)* .... (GBR)

Shingo Kunieda [1] — 4/6 7/5 7/6(5)

THE GENTLEMEN'S WHEELCHAIR DOUBLES 2022
Holders: ALFIE HEWETT (GBR) & GORDON REID (GBR)

The Champions will become the holders, for the year only, of a Cup presented by The All England Lawn Tennis and Croquet Club. The Champions will receive a three-quarter size replica of the Cup. A Silver Salver will be presented to each of the Runners-up.
The matches will be the best of three tie-break sets.

Final

1. **Alfie Hewett** (GBR) & **Gordon Reid** (GBR) .... [1]
    Alfie Hewett & Gordon Reid [1] .... 6/3 1/6 7/6(7)

2. Tom Egberink (NED) & Joachim Gerard (BEL) ....

3. Tokito Oda (JPN) & Nicolas Peifer (FRA) ....
    Gustavo Fernandez & Shingo Kunieda [2] 6/4 6/2

4. **Gustavo Fernandez** (ARG) & **Shingo Kunieda** (JPN) .... [2]

Gustavo Fernandez & Shingo Kunieda [2] — 6/3 6/1

THE LADIES' WHEELCHAIR SINGLES 2022
Holder: DIEDE DE GROOT (NED)

The Champion will become the holder, for the year only, of a Cup presented by The All England Lawn Tennis and Croquet Club. The Champion will receive a three-quarter size replica of the Cup. A Silver Salver will be presented to the Runner-up.
The matches will be the best of three tie-break sets.

First Round   Semi-final   Final

1. **Diede De Groot [1]** *(1)* .... (NED)
    Diede De Groot [1] 6/1 6/1

2. Dana Mathewson *(9)* .... (USA)
    Diede De Groot [1] 6/1 6/0

3. Lucy Shuker *(7)* .... (GBR)
    Momoko Ohtani 6/2 6/2

(WC) 4. Momoko Ohtani *(6)* .... (JPN)

5. Aniek Van Koot *(3)* .... (NED)
    Jiske Griffioen 6/2 6/2

6. Jiske Griffioen *(5)* .... (NED)
    Yui Kamiji [2] 6/1 6/2

7. Kgothatso Montjane *(4)* .... (RSA)
    Yui Kamiji [2] 6/3 6/3

8. **Yui Kamiji [2]** *(2)* .... (JPN)

Diede De Groot [1] — 6/4 6/2

THE LADIES' WHEELCHAIR DOUBLES 2022
Holders: YUI KAMIJI (JPN) & JORDANNE WHILEY (GBR)

The Champions will become the holders, for the year only, of a Cup presented by The All England Lawn Tennis and Croquet Club. The Champions will receive a three-quarter size replica of the Cup. A Silver Salver will be presented to each of the Runners-up.
The matches will be the best of three tie-break sets.

Final

1. **Diede De Groot** (NED) & **Aniek Van Koot** (NED) .... [1]
    Diede De Groot & Aniek Van Koot [1] 7/5 7/5

2. Jiske Griffioen (NED) & Momoko Ohtani (JPN) ....

3. Yui Kamiji (JPN) & Dana Mathewson (USA) ....
    Yui Kamiji & Dana Mathewson 6/4 6/2

4. **Kgothatso Montjane** (RSA) & **Lucy Shuker** (GBR) .... [2]

Yui Kamiji & Dana Mathewson — 6/1 7/5

Heavy type denotes seeded players. The figure in brackets against names denotes the order in which they have been seeded.
(A)=Alternates. (WC)=Wild cards.

THE QUAD WHEELCHAIR SINGLES 2022
Holder: DYLAN ALCOTT (AUS)

The Champion will become the holder, for the year only, of a Cup presented by The All England Lawn Tennis and Croquet Club. The Champion will receive a three-quarter size replica of the Cup. A Silver Salver will be presented to the Runner-up.
The matches will be the best of three sets. If the score should reach 6-6 in the final set, the match will be decided by a tie-break.

First Round	Semi-final	Final

1. **Niels Vink [1]** *(1)* .... (NED)
   Niels Vink [1] 6/1 6/1
(WC) 2. Ymanitu Silva *(8)* .... (BRA)

3. Andy Lapthorne *(3)* .... (GBR)
   Heath Davidson 6/1 6/3
4. Heath Davidson *(5)* .... (AUS)

Niels Vink [1] .... 7/6(7) 6/1

5. Donald Ramphadi *(7)* .... (RSA)
   David Wagner 6/1 6/3
6. David Wagner *(4)* .... (USA)

7. Koji Sugeno *(6)* .... (JPN)
   Sam Schroder [2] 6/4 0/6 6/0
8. **Sam Schroder [2]** *(2)* .... (NED)

Sam Schroder [2] .... 6/0 6/7(5) 6/1

Sam Schroder [2] 7/6(5) 6/1

THE QUAD WHEELCHAIR DOUBLES 2022
Holders: ANDY LAPTHORNE (GBR) & DAVID WAGNER (USA)

The Champion will become the holder, for the year only, of a Cup presented by The All England Lawn Tennis and Croquet Club. The Champion will receive a three-quarter size replica of the Cup. A Silver Salver will be presented to the Runner-up.
The matches will be the best of three sets. If the score should reach 6-6 in the final set, the match will be decided by a tie-break.

	Final

1. **Sam Schroder** (NED) & **Niels Vink** (NED)...[1]
   Sam Schroder & Niels Vink [1] 6/2 6/2
2. Heath Davidson (AUS) & Ymanitu Silva (BRA) ....

3. Donald Ramphadi (RSA) & Koji Sugeno (JPN) ....
   Andy Lapthorne & David Wagner [2] .... 6/3 3/4 Ret'd
4. **Andy Lapthorne** (GBR) & **David Wagner** (USA) ....[2]

Sam Schroder & Niels Vink [1] 6/7(4) 6/2 6/3

Heavy type denotes seeded players. The figure in brackets against names denotes the order in which they have been seeded.
(A)=Alternates. (WC)=Wild cards.

*Sam Schroder (**right**) and Niels Vink in action against Andy Lapthorne and David Wagner in the Quad Wheelchair Doubles Final on No.1 Court*

THE 18&U BOYS' SINGLES CHAMPIONSHIP 2022
Holder: AMIR BANERJEE (USA)

The Champion will become the holder, for the year only, of a Cup presented by The All England Lawn Tennis and Croquet Club.
The Champion will receive a three-quarter size Cup and the Runner-up will receive a Silver Salver. The matches will be the best of three sets. If the score should reach 6-6 in the final set, the match will be decided by a first-to-ten tie-break.

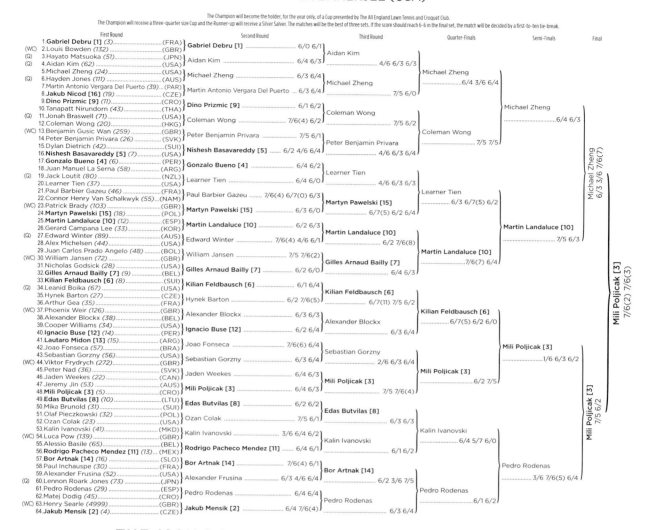

THE 18&U BOYS' DOUBLES CHAMPIONSHIP 2022
Holders: EDAS BUTVILAS (LTU) & ALEJANDRO MANZANERA PERTUSA (ESP)

The Champions will become the holders, for the year only, of a Cup presented by The All England Lawn Tennis and Croquet Club. The Champions will receive a three-quarter size Cup and the Runners-up will receive Silver Salvers.
The matches will be the best of three sets. If the score should reach 6-6 in the final set, the match will be decided by a first-to-ten tie-break.

Heavy type denotes seeded players. The figure in brackets against names denotes the order in which they have been seeded. The Committee reserves the right to alter the seeding order in the event of withdrawals.
(WC)=Wild cards. (A)=Alternates.

THE 18&U GIRLS' SINGLES CHAMPIONSHIP 2022
Holder: ANE MINTEGI DEL OLMO (ESP)

The Champion will become the holder, for the year only, of a Cup presented by The All England Lawn Tennis and Croquet Club.
The Champion will receive a three-quarter size Cup and the Runner-up will receive a Silver Salver. The matches will be the best of three sets. If the score should reach 6-6 in the final set, the match will be decided by a first-to-ten tie-break.

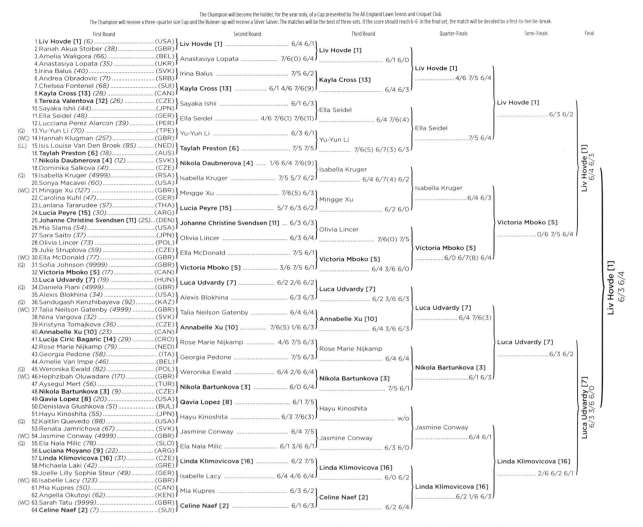

First Round

1. Liv Hovde [1] (6) ....(USA)
2. Ranah Akua Stoiber (38) ....(GBR)
3. Amelia Waligora (66) ....(BEL)
4. Anastasiya Lopata (35) ....(UKR)
5. Irina Balus (40) ....(SVK)
6. Andrea Obradovic (71) ....(SRB)
7. Chelsea Fontenel (68) ....(SUI)
8. Kayla Cross [13] (28) ....(CAN)
9. Tereza Valentova [12] (26) ....(CZE)
10. Sayaka Ishii (44) ....(JPN)
11. Ella Seidel (48) ....(GER)
12. Lucciana Perez Alarcon (39) ....(PER)
(Q) 13. Yu-Yun Li (70) ....(TPE)
(WC) 14. Hannah Klugman (257) ....(GBR)
(LL) 15. Isis Louise Van Den Broek (85) ...(NED)
16. Taylah Preston [6] (18) ....(AUS)
17. Nikola Daubnerova [4] (12) ....(SVK)
18. Dominika Salkova (41) ....(CZE)
(Q) 19. Isabella Kruger (4999) ....(RSA)
20. Sonya Macavei (60) ....(USA)
(WC) 21. Mingge Xu (127) ....(GBR)
22. Carolina Kuhl (47) ....(GER)
23. Lanlana Tararudee (57) ....(THA)
24. Lucia Peyre [15] (30) ....(ARG)
25. Johanne Christine Svendsen [11] (25)...(DEN)
26. Mia Slama (54) ....(USA)
27. Sara Saito (37) ....(JPN)
28. Olivia Lincer (73) ....(POL)
29. Julie Struplova (59) ....(CZE)
(WC) 30. Ella McDonald (77) ....(GBR)
(Q) 31. Sofia Johnson (9999) ....(GBR)
32. Victoria Mboko [5] (17) ....(CAN)
33. Luca Udvardy [7] (19) ....(HUN)
(Q) 34. Daniela Piani (4999) ....(GBR)
35. Alexis Blokhina (34) ....(USA)
(Q) 36. Sandugash Kenzhibayeva (92) ...(KAZ)
(WC) 37. Talia Neilson Gatenby (4999) ...(GBR)
38. Nina Vargova (32) ....(SVK)
39. Kristyna Tomajkova (36) ....(CZE)
40. Annabelle Xu [10] (23) ....(CAN)
41. Lucija Ciric Bagaric [14] (29) ......(CRO)
42. Rose Marie Nijkamp (79) ....(NED)
43. Georgia Pedone (58) ....(ITA)
44. Amelie Van Impe (46) ....(BEL)
(Q) 45. Weronika Ewald (82) ....(POL)
(WC) 46. Hephzibah Oluwadare (171) ...(GBR)
47. Aysegul Mert (56) ....(TUR)
48. Nikola Bartunkova [3] (9) ....(CZE)
49. Qavia Lopez [8] (20) ....(USA)
50. Denislava Glushkova (51) ....(BUL)
51. Hayu Kinoshita (55) ....(JPN)
(Q) 52. Kaitlin Quevedo (88) ....(USA)
53. Renata Jamrichova (67) ....(SVK)
(WC) 54. Jasmine Conway (4999) ....(GBR)
(Q) 55. Ela Nala Milic (78) ....(SLO)
56. Luciana Moyano [9] (22) ....(ARG)
57. Linda Klimovicova [16] (31) ....(CZE)
58. Michaela Laki (42) ....(GRE)
59. Joelle Lilly Sophie Steur (49) ....(GER)
(WC) 60. Isabelle Lacy (123) ....(GBR)
61. Mia Kupres (50) ....(CAN)
62. Angella Okutoyi (62) ....(KEN)
(WC) 63. Sarah Tatu (9999) ....(GBR)
64. Celine Naef [2] (7) ....(SUI)

Second Round

Liv Hovde [1] 6/4 6/1
Anastasiya Lopata .... 7/6(3) 6/4
Irina Balus 7/5 6/2
Kayla Cross [13] .... 6/1 4/6 7/6(9)
Sayaka Ishii 6/1 6/3
Ella Seidel .... 4/6 7/6(1) 7/6(11)
Yu-Yun Li 6/3 6/1
Taylah Preston [6] 7/5 7/5
Nikola Daubnerova [4] ..... 1/6 6/4 7/6(9)
Isabella Kruger 7/5 5/7 6/2
Mingge Xu .... 7/6(5) 6/3
Lucia Peyre [15] 5/7 6/3 6/2
Johanne Christine Svendsen [11] ... 6/3 6/3
Olivia Lincer 6/3 6/4
Ella McDonald 7/5 6/1
Victoria Mboko [5] 3/6 7/5 6/1
Luca Udvardy [7] 6/2 2/6 6/2
Alexis Blokhina 6/3 6/3
Talia Neilson Gatenby 6/4 6/4
Annabelle Xu [10] .... 7/6(5) 1/6 6/3
Rose Marie Nijkamp 4/6 7/5 6/3
Georgia Pedone 7/5 6/3
Weronika Ewald 6/4 2/6 6/4
Nikola Bartunkova [3] 6/0 6/4
Qavia Lopez [8] 6/1 7/5
Hayu Kinoshita .... 6/3 7/6(3)
Jasmine Conway 6/4 7/5
Ela Nala Milic 6/1 3/6 6/1
Linda Klimovicova [16] 6/2 7/5
Isabelle Lacy 6/4 4/6 6/4
Mia Kupres 6/3 6/2
Celine Naef [2] 6/1 6/3

Third Round

Liv Hovde [1] 6/1 6/0
Kayla Cross [13] 6/4 6/3
Ella Seidel .... 6/4 7/6(4)
Yu-Yun Li .... 7/6(5) 6/7(3) 6/3
Isabella Kruger ...... 6/4 6/7(4) 6/2
Mingge Xu 6/2 6/0
Olivia Lincer .... 7/6(0) 7/5
Victoria Mboko [5] ... 6/0 6/7(8) 6/4
Luca Udvardy [7] 6/2 3/6 6/2
Annabelle Xu [10] 6/4 3/6 6/3
Rose Marie Nijkamp 6/4 6/4
Nikola Bartunkova [3] 7/5 6/1
Hayu Kinoshita .... w/o
Jasmine Conway 6/3 6/0
Linda Klimovicova [16] 6/0 6/2
Celine Naef [2] 6/2 6/4

Quarter-Finals

Liv Hovde [1] 4/6 7/5 6/4
Isabella Kruger 7/5 6/4
Victoria Mboko [5] .... 6/0 6/7(8) 6/4
Luca Udvardy [7] .... 6/4 7/6(3)
Nikola Bartunkova [3] 6/1 6/3
Jasmine Conway 6/4 6/1
Linda Klimovicova [16] 6/2 1/6 6/3

Semi-Finals

Liv Hovde [1] 6/3 6/2
Victoria Mboko [5] 0/6 7/5 6/4
Luca Udvardy [7] 6/3 6/2
Linda Klimovicova [16] ... 2/6 6/2 6/1

Final

Liv Hovde [1]
6/4 6/3

Liv Hovde [1]
6/3 6/4

Luca Udvardy [7]
6/3 3/6 6/0

Liv Hovde [1]
6/3 6/4

THE 18&U GIRLS' DOUBLES CHAMPIONSHIP 2022
Holders: KRISTINA DMITRUK (BLR) & DIANA SHNAIDER (RUS)

The Champions will become the holders, for the year only, of a Cup presented by The All England Lawn Tennis and Croquet Club. The Champions will receive a three-quarter size Cup and the Runners-up will receive Silver Salvers.
The matches will be the best of three sets. If the score should reach 6-6 in the final set, the match will be decided by a first-to-ten tie-break.

First Round

1. Nikola Bartunkova (CZE) & Celine Naef (SUI) .... [1]
2. Carolina Kuhl (GER) & Tereza Valentova (CZE) ....
3. Sofia Johnson (GBR) & Daniela Piani (GBR) ....
4. Renata Jamrichova (SVK) & Olivia Lincer (POL) ....
(WC) 5. Hannah Klugman (GBR) & Hephzibah Oluwadare (GBR) ...
6. Weronika Ewald (POL) & Isis Louise Van Den Broek (NED) ...
7. Sonya Macavei (USA) & Julie Struplova (CZE) ....
8. Alexis Blokhina (USA) & Luca Udvardy (HUN) .... [5]
9. Kayla Cross (CAN) & Victoria Mboko (CAN) .... [4]
10. Sandugash Kenzhibayeva (KAZ) & Zhanel Rustemova (KAZ) ...
11. Ella Seidel (GER) & Joelle Lilly Sophie Steur (GER) .....
12. Anastasiya Lopata (UKR) & Aysegul Mert (TUR) ....
(A) 13. Jessica Matthews (GBR) & Jaquelyn Ogunwale (GBR) ...
14. Chelsea Fontenel (SUI) & Johanne Christine Svendsen (DEN) ...
(WC) 15. Talia Neilson Gatenby (GBR) & Mingge Xu (GBR) ...
16. Kristyna Tomajkova (CZE) & Nina Vargova (SVK) ... [8]
17. Luciana Moyano (ARG) & Lucciana Perez Alarcon (PER) ... [7]
18. Sayaka Ishii (JPN) & Lanlana Tararudee (THA) ....
19. Andrea Obradovic (SRB) & Aruzhan Sagandikova (KAZ) ...
20. Annabelle Xu (CAN) & Naomi Xu (CAN) ....
(WC) 21. Isabelle Lacy (GBR) & Ella McDonald (GBR) ....
22. Yu-Yun Li (TPE) & Sara Saito (JPN) ....
23. Amelie Van Impe (BEL) & Amelia Waligora (BEL) ....
24. Lucija Ciric Bagaric (CRO) & Nikola Daubnerova (SVK) ... [3]
25. Irina Balus (SVK) & Taylah Preston (AUS) .... [6]
26. Linda Klimovicova (CZE) & Dominika Salkova (CZE) ......
(WC) 27. Given Roach (GBR) & Millie Skelton (GBR) ....
28. Lucia Peyre (ARG) & Mia Slama (USA) ....
29. Rose Marie Nijkamp (NED) & Angella Okutoyi (KEN) ......
30. Georgia Pedone (ITA) & Kaitlin Quevedo (USA) ....
31. Denislava Glushkova (BUL) & Hayu Kinoshita (JPN) ......
32. Liv Hovde (USA) & Qavia Lopez (USA) .... [2]

Second Round

Nikola Bartunkova & Celine Naef [1] 6/3 6/4
Renata Jamrichova & Olivia Lincer 6/3 6/1
Hannah Klugman & Hephzibah Oluwadare... 6/3 4/6 10-7
Sonya Macavei & Julie Struplova 5/7 6/3 10-2
Kayla Cross & Victoria Mboko [4] 6/3 6/3
Ella Seidel & Joelle Lilly Sophie Steur... 6/2 4/6 10-5
Chelsea Fontenel & Johanne Christine Svendsen ... 3/6 6/2 10-8
Kristyna Tomajkova & Nina Vargova [8] 6/4 6/4
Sayaka Ishii & Lanlana Tararudee.... 1/6 7/6(2) 12-10
Annabelle Xu & Naomi Xu................. 2/6 6/3 10-7
Yu-Yun Li & Sara Saito 6/4 6/4
Lucija Ciric Bagaric & Nikola Daubnerova [3] ... 1/6 7/5 10-3
Linda Klimovicova & Dominika Salkova......... w/o
Lucia Peyre & Mia Slama .... 6/4 7/6(6)
Rose Marie Nijkamp & Angella Okutoyi.. 6/4 6/4
Denislava Glushkova & Hayu Kinoshita......... w/o

Quarter-Finals

Nikola Bartunkova & Celine Naef [1] ... 4/6 6/3 10-4
Hannah Klugman & Hephzibah Oluwadare ... 6/4 6/3
Kayla Cross & Victoria Mboko [4] ... 6/4 6/3
Kristyna Tomajkova & Nina Vargova [8] ... 3/6 6/4 10-6
Sayaka Ishii & Lanlana Tararudee ... 6/0 6/1
Lucija Ciric Bagaric & Nikola Daubnerova [3] ... 6/3 7/6(5)
Linda Klimovicova & Dominika Salkova ... 3/6 7/5 15-13
Rose Marie Nijkamp & Angella Okutoyi ... 6/2 6/3

Semi-Finals

Nikola Bartunkova & Celine Naef [1] ... 6/0 6/1
Kayla Cross & Victoria Mboko [4] ... 1/6 7/5 13-11
Lucija Ciric Bagaric & Nikola Daubnerova [3] ... 6/2 7/6(3)
Rose Marie Nijkamp & Angella Okutoyi ... 6/7(5) 6/4 11-9

Final

Kayla Cross & Victoria Mboko [4]
6/4 6/4

Rose Marie Nijkamp & Angella Okutoyi
3/6 6/4 11-9

Rose Marie Nijkamp & Angella Okutoyi
3/6 6/4 11-9

Heavy type denotes seeded players. The figure in brackets against names denotes the order in which they have been seeded. The Committee reserves the right to alter the seeding order in the event of withdrawals.
(WC)=Wild cards. (A)=Alternates.

THE 14&U BOYS' SINGLES CHAMPIONSHIP 2022
INAUGURAL EVENT

The Champion will become the holder, for the year only, of a Cup presented by The All England Lawn Tennis and Croquet Club.
The Champion will receive a three-quarter size Cup and the Runner-up will receive a Silver Salver. The matches will be the best of three sets. If a match should reach one set all a 10-point tie-break will replace the third set.

GROUP A	Ivan Ivanov (BUL) [1]	Dante Pagani (ARG)	Ali Missoum (MAR)	Mark Ceban (GBR) [8]	Wins	Losses	Group Winner
Ivan Ivanov (BUL) [1]		4/6 6/3 [10-8] W	1/6 6/1 [10-5] W	6/4 6/4 W	3	0	Ivan Ivanov (BUL) [1]
Dante Pagani (ARG)	6/4 3/6 [8-10] L		6/2 6/1 W	3/6 2/6 L	1	2	
Ali Missoum (MAR)	6/1 1/6 [5-10] L	2/6 1/6 L		6/4 1/6 [6-10] L	0	3	
Mark Ceban (GBR) [8]	4/6 4/6 L	6/3 6/2 W	4/6 6/1 [10-6] W		2	1	

GROUP B	Matei Todoran (ROU) [2]	Benjamin Chelia (ARG)	La Hunn Lam (NMI)	Keaton Hance (USA) [7]	Wins	Losses	Group Winner
Matei Todoran (ROU) [2]		6/2 6/2 W	6/1 6/2 W	3/6 6/3 [10-4] W	3	0	Matei Todoran (ROU) [2]
Benjamin Chelia (ARG)	2/6 2/6 L		6/1 6/0 W	0/6 0/6 L	1	2	
La Hunn Lam (NMI)	1/6 2/6 L	1/6 0/6 L		0/6 0/6 L	0	3	
Keaton Hance (USA) [7]	6/3 3/6 [4-10] L	6/0 6/0 W	6/0 6/0 W		2	1	

GROUP C	Carel Aubriel Ngounoue (USA) [3]	Malek Alqurneh (JOR)	Pedro Dietrich (BRA)	Jake Dembo (AUS) [6]	Wins	Losses	Group Winner
Carel Aubriel Ngounoue (USA) [3]		6/0 6/0 W	6/3 6/2 W	6/0 6/1 W	3	0	Carel Aubriel Ngounoue (USA) [3]
Malek Alqurneh (JOR)	0/6 0/6 L		6/3 3/6 [10-3] W	0/6 3/6 L	1	2	
Pedro Dietrich (BRA)	3/6 2/6 L	3/6 6/3 [3-10] L		1/6 4/6 L	0	3	
Jake Dembo (AUS) [6]	0/6 1/6 L	6/0 6/3 W	6/1 6/4 W		2	1	

GROUP D	Maximilian Heidlmair (AUT) [4]	Liam Channon (GBR)	Mauricio Schtulmann (MEX)	Se Hyuk Cho (KOR) [5]	Wins	Losses	Group Winner
Maximilian Heidlmair (AUT) [4]		6/1 6/4 L	6/1 6/3 W	1/6 1/6 L	2	1	Se Hyuk Cho (KOR) [5]
Liam Channon (GBR)	1/6 4/6 W		6/4 7/6(4) W	0/6 6/7(2) L	1	2	
Mauricio Schtulmann (MEX)	1/6 3/6 L	4/6 6/7(4) L		2/6 3/6 L	0	3	
Se Hyuk Cho (KOR) [5]	6/1 6/1 W	6/0 7/6(2) W	6/2 6/3 W		3	0	

Semi-Finals   **Final**   **Champion**

Ivan Ivanov (BUL) .... [1]

Se Hyuk Cho [5]

Se Hyuk Cho (KOR) .... [5] .... 7/6(5) 1/6 [11-9]

Se Hyuk Cho [5] .... 7/6(5) 6/3

Carel Aubriel Ngounoue (USA) .... [3]

Carel Aubriel Ngounoue [3]

Matei Todoran (ROU) .... [2] .... 3/6 6/4 [11-9]

THE 14&U BOYS' SINGLES CONSOLATION PLAY-OFFS

Consolation Play-Off for 5th/6th Position (2nd placed players from round robin groups)

Maximilian Heidlmair (AUT) ....

Mark Ceban

Mark Ceban (GBR) 6/4 6/0

Mark Ceban 6/3 6/2

Jake Dembo (AUS) ....

Jake Dembo

Keaton Hance (USA) .... w/o

Consolation Play-Off for 9th/10th Position (3rd placed players from round robin groups)

Liam Channon (GBR) ....

Dante Pagani

Dante Pagani (ARG) .... 6/4 5/7 [10-5]

Dante Pagani 6/4 6/4

Malek Alqurneh (JOR) ....

Benjamin Chelia

Benjamin Chelia (ARG) 6/1 6/3

Consolation Play-Off for 13th/14th Position (4th placed players from round robin groups)

Mauricio Schtulmann (MEX) ....

Ali Missoum

Ali Missoum (MAR) .... 7/6(6) 4/6 [12-10]

Ali Missoum .... 6/2 7/6(0)

Pedro Dietrich (BRA) ....

Pedro Dietrich

La Hunn Lam (NMI) 6/0 6/0

THE 14&U GIRLS' SINGLES CHAMPIONSHIP 2022
INAUGURAL EVENT

The Champion will become the holder, for the year only, of a Cup presented by The All England Lawn Tennis and Croquet Club.
The Champion will receive a three-quarter size Cup and the Runner-up will receive a Silver Salver. The matches will be the best of three sets. If a match should reach one set all a 10-point tie-break will replace the third set.

GROUP A	Alexia Ioana Tatu (ROU) [1]	Giselle Isabella Guillen (AUS)	Marianne Angel (MEX)	Arabella Loftus (GBR) [7]	Wins	Losses	Group Winner
Alexia Ioana Tatu (ROU) [1]		6/2 6/4 W	3/6 6/0 [10-2] W	6/1 6/0 W	3	0	Alexia Ioana Tatu (ROU) [1]
Giselle Isabella Guillen (AUS)	2/6 4/6 L		6/1 6/4 W	6/2 6/0 W	2	1	
Marianne Angel (MEX)	6/3 0/6 [2-10] L	1/6 4/6 L		2/6 5/7 L	0	3	
Arabella Loftus (GBR) [7]	1/6 0/6 L	2/6 0/6 L	6/2 7/5 W		1	2	

GROUP B	Veronika Sekerkova (CZE) [2]	Candela Vazquez (ARG)	Isabelle Britton (GBR)	Maria Badache (ALG) [8]	Wins	Losses	Group Winner
Veronika Sekerkova (CZE) [2]		6/1 4/6 [6-10] L	2/6 7/6(5) [5-10] L	6/4 1/0 Ret'd W	1	2	Isabelle Britton (GBR)
Candela Vazquez (ARG)	1/6 6/4 [10-6] W		3/6 6/3 [7-10] L	6/4 6/7(4) [5-10] L	1	2	
Isabelle Britton (GBR)	6/2 6/7(5) [10-5] W	6/3 3/6 [10-7] W		6/2 6/0 W	3	0	
Maria Badache (ALG) [8]	4/6 0/1 Ret'd L	4/6 7/6(4) [10-5] W	2/6 0/6 L		1	2	

GROUP C	Mika Stojsavljevic (GBR) [3]	Aishwarya Jadhav (IND)	Aishi Das (NZL)	Andreea Diana Soare (ROU) [5]	Wins	Losses	Group Winner
Mika Stojsavljevic (GBR) [3]		6/4 6/1 W	6/2 7/6(3) W	6/1 4/6 [3-10] L	2	1	Andreea Diana Soare (ROU) [5]
Aishwarya Jadhav (IND)	4/6 1/6 L		3/6 6/2 [5-10] L	3/6 2/6 L	0	3	
Aishi Das (NZL)	2/6 6/7(3) L	6/3 2/6 [10-5] W		4/6 4/6 L	1	2	
Andreea Diana Soare (ROU) [5]	1/6 6/4 [10-3] W	6/3 6/2 W	6/4 6/4 W		3	0	

GROUP D	Nicole Okhtenberg (USA) [4]	Azuna Ichioka (JPN)	Sol Ailin Larraya Guidi (ARG)	Scarlette Hetherington (FRA) [6]	Wins	Losses	Group Winner
Nicole Okhtenberg (USA) [4]		2/6 3/6 L	1/6 5/7 L	6/0 5/7 [10-6] W	1	2	Sol Ailin Larraya Guidi (ARG)
Azuna Ichioka (JPN)	6/2 6/3 W		4/6 6/4 [8-10] L	6/2 6/2 W	2	1	
Sol Ailin Larraya Guidi (ARG)	6/1 7/5 W	6/4 4/6 [10-8] W		7/5 6/3 W	3	0	
Scarlette Hetherington (FRA) [6]	0/6 7/5 [6-10] L	2/6 2/6 L	5/7 3/6 L		0	3	

Semi-Finals

Alexia Ioana Tatu (ROU) ...... [1]
Sol Ailin Larraya Guidi (ARG) ......

Andreea Diana Soare (ROU) ...... [5]
Isabelle Britton (GBR) ......

Final

Alexia Ioana Tatu [1] 6/0 6/3
Andreea Diana Soare [5] 6/0 7/5

Champion

Alexia Ioana Tatu [1] ...... 7/6(2) 6/4

THE 14&U GIRLS' SINGLES CONSOLATION PLAY-OFFS

Consolation Play-Off for 5th/6th Position (2nd placed players from round robin groups)

Mika Stojsavljevc (GBR) ......
Veronika Sekerkova (CZE) ......
Mika Stojsavljevic ...... 6/0 2/6 [10-7]

Azuna Ichioka (JPN) ......
Giselle Isabella Guillen (AUS) ......
Giselle Isabella Guillen 6/4 6/3

Mika Stojsavljevic 6/2 6/3

Consolation Play-Off for 9th/10th Position (3rd placed players from round robin groups)

Aishi Das (NZL) ......
Candela Vazquez (ARG) ......
Aishi Das ...... w/o

Nicole Okhtenberg (USA) ......
Arabella Loftus (GBR) ......
Nicole Okhtenberg 6/2 6/2

Nicole Okhtenberg ...... 1/6 6/4 [10-8]

Consolation Play-Off for 13th/14th Position (4th placed players from round robin groups)

Aishwarya Jadhav (IND) ......
Maria Badache (ALG) ......
Aishwarya Jadhav ...... w/o

Scarlette Hetherington (FRA) ......
Marianne Angel (MEX) ......
Scarlette Hetherington ...... 4/6 6/1 [10-5]

Scarlette Hetherington 6/4 6/1

THE GENTLEMEN'S INVITATION DOUBLES 2022
Holders: ARNAUD CLEMENT (FRA) & MICHAEL LLODRA (FRA) EVENT LAST HELD IN 2019

The Champions will become the holders, for the year only, of a Cup presented by The All England Lawn Tennis and Croquet Club. The Champions will receive a silver three-quarter size Cup. A Silver Medal will be presented to each of the Runners-up.
The matches will be the best of three sets. If a match should reach one set all a 10-point tie-break will replace the third set.

GROUP A	Marcos Baghdatis (CYP) & Xavier Malisse, (BEL)	James Blake (USA) & Daniel Nestor, (CAN)	Arnaud Clement (FRA) & Michael Llodra (FRA)	Tommy Haas (GER) & Mark Philippoussis (AUS)	Wins	Losses	Final
Marcos Baghdatis (CYP) & Xavier Malisse, (BEL)		6/2 7/6(9) W	2/6 7/6(3) [10-7] W	2/6 6/4 [10-6] W	3	0	
James Blake (USA) & Daniel Nestor, (CAN)	2/6 6/7(9) L		3/6 4/6 L	1/6 6/7(5) L	0	3	
Arnaud Clement (FRA) & Michael Llodra (FRA)	6/2 6/7(3) [7-10] L	6/3 6/4 W		4/6 5/7 L	1	2	Marcos Baghdatis (CYP) & Xavier Malisse, (BEL)
Tommy Haas (GER) & Mark Philippoussis (AUS)	6/2 4/6 [6-10] L	6/1 7/6(5) W	6/4 7/5 W		2	1	

GROUP B	Bob Bryan (USA) & Mike Bryan (USA)	Fernando Gonzalez (CHI) & Sebastien Grosjean (FRA)	Jonathan Marray (GBR) & Frederik Nielsen (DEN)	Jurgen Melzer (AUT) & Gilles Muller (LUX)	Wins	Losses	Final
Bob Bryan (USA) & Mike Bryan (USA)		6/4 6/4 W	6/4 6/4 W	7/6(5) 6/2 W	3	0	
Fernando Gonzalez (CHI) & Sebastien Grosjean (FRA)	4/6 4/6 L		6/3 7/5 W	7/5 2/6 [4-10] L	1	2	Bob Bryan (USA) & Mike Bryan (USA)
Jonathan Marray (GBR) & Frederik Nielsen (DEN)	4/6 4/6 L	3/6 5/7 L		6/7(3) 4/6 L	0	3	
Jurgen Melzer (AUT) & Gilles Muller (LUX)	6/7(5) 2/6 L	5/7 6/2 [10-4] W	7/6(3) 6/4 W		2	1	

Final: Bob Bryan (USA) & Mike Bryan (USA) 6/3 6/4

THE LADIES' INVITATION DOUBLES 2022
Holders: CARA BLACK (ZIM) & MARTINA NAVRATILOVA (USA) EVENT LAST HELD IN 2019

The Champions will become the holders, for the year only, of a Cup presented by The All England Lawn Tennis and Croquet Club. The Champions will receive a silver three-quarter size Cup. A Silver Medal will be presented to each of the Runners-up.
The matches will be the best of three sets. If a match should reach one set all a 10-point tie-break will replace the third set.

GROUP A	Kim Clijsters (BEL) & Martina Hingis (SUI)	Nathalie Dechy (FRA) & Barbara Schett (AUT)	Anna-Lena Groenefeld (GER) & Karolina Sprem (CRO)	Vania King (USA) & Yaroslava Shvedova (KAZ)	Wins	Losses	Final
Kim Clijsters (BEL) & Martina Hingis (SUI)		6/0 6/3 W	6/1 6/3 W	6/4 6/1 W	3	0	
Nathalie Dechy (FRA) & Barbara Schett (AUT)	0/6 3/6 L		4/6 3/6 L	2/6 4/6 L	0	3	
Anna-Lena Groenefeld (GER) & Karolina Sprem (CRO)	1/6 3/6 L	6/4 6/3 W		6/3 6/7(4) [7-10] L	1	2	Kim Clijsters (BEL) & Martina Hingis (SUI)
Vania King (USA) & Yaroslava Shvedova (KAZ)	4/6 1/6 L	6/2 6/4 W	3/6 7/6(4) [10-7] W		2	1	

GROUP B	Casey Dellacqua (AUS) & Alicia Molik (AUS)	Daniela Hantuchova (SVK) & Laura Robson (GBR)	Jelena Jankovic (SRB) & Agnieszka Radwanska (POL)	Flavia Pennetta (ITA) & Francesca Schiavone (ITA)	Wins	Losses	Final
Casey Dellacqua (AUS) & Alicia Molik (AUS)		3/6 5/7 L	2/6 2/6 L	7/6(3) 3/6 [5-10] L	0	3	
Daniela Hantuchova (SVK) & Laura Robson (GBR)	6/3 7/5 W		6/4 6/2 W	5/7 5/7 L	2	1	Daniela Hantuchova (SVK) & Laura Robson (GBR)
Jelena Jankovic (SRB) & Agnieszka Radwanska (POL)	6/2 6/2 W	4/6 2/6 L		6/4 6/3 W	2	1	
Flavia Pennetta (ITA) & Francesca Schiavone (ITA)	6/7(5) 6/3 [10-5] W	7/5 7/5 W	4/6 3/6 L		2	1	

Final: Kim Clijsters (BEL) & Martina Hingis (SUI) 6/4 6/2

THE MIXED INVITATION DOUBLES 2022
INAUGURAL EVENT

The Champions will become the holders, for the year only, of a Cup presented by The All England Lawn Tennis and Croquet Club. The Champions will receive a silver three-quarter size Cup. A Silver Medal will be presented to each of the Runners-up.
The matches will be the best of three sets. If a match should reach one set all a 10-point tie-break will replace the third set.

GROUP A	Mansour Bahrami (FRA) & Conchita Martinez (ESP)	Thomas Enqvist (SWE) & Rennae Stubbs (AUS)	Thomas Johansson (SWE) & Mary Joe Fernandez (USA)	Todd Woodbridge (AUS) & Cara Black (ZIM)	Wins	Losses	Final
Mansour Bahrami (FRA) & Conchita Martinez (ESP)		4/6 6/4 [7-10] L	6/4 6/4 W	6/7(2) 1/6 L	1	2	
Thomas Enqvist (SWE) & Rennae Stubbs (AUS)	6/4 4/6 [10-7] W		6/4 2/6 [16-14] W	3/6 4/6 L	2	1	
Thomas Johansson (SWE) & Mary Joe Fernandez (USA)	4/6 4/6 L	4/6 6/2 [14-16] L		4/6 3/6 L	0	3	Todd Woodbridge (AUS) & Cara Black (ZIM)
Todd Woodbridge (AUS) & Cara Black (ZIM)	7/6(2) 6/1 W	6/3 6/4 W	6/4 6/3 W		3	0	

GROUP B	Goran Ivanisevic (CRO) & Mary Pierce (FRA)	Greg Rusedski (GBR) & Anne Keothavong (GBR)	Mark Woodforde (AUS) & Iva Majoli (CRO)	Nenad Zimonjic (SRB) & Marion Bartoli (FRA)	Wins	Losses	Final
Goran Ivanisevic (CRO) & Mary Pierce (FRA)		6/7(6) 6/3 [10-6] W	3/6 6/7(5) L	4/6 4/6 L	1	2	
Greg Rusedski (GBR) & Anne Keothavong (GBR)	7/6(6) 3/6 [6-10] L		4/6 6/7(7) L	3/6 4/6 L	0	3	
Mark Woodforde (AUS) & Iva Majoli (CRO)	6/3 7/6(5) W	6/4 7/6(7) W		2/6 7/6(7) [10-12] L	2	1	Nenad Zimonjic (SRB) & Marion Bartoli (FRA)
Nenad Zimonjic (SRB) & Marion Bartoli (FRA)	6/4 6/4 W	6/3 6/4 *Martina Hingis stood in for Bartoli for this match only* W	6/2 6/7(7) [12-10] W		3	0	

Final: Nenad Zimonjic (SRB) & Marion Bartoli (FRA) 7/6(1) 6/1

These events consists of eight invited pairs divided into two groups, playing each other within their group on a 'round robin' basis. The group winner is the pair with the highest number of wins.
In the case of a tie the winning pair may be determined by head to head results or a formula based on percentage of sets/games won to those played.

THE ROLLS OF HONOUR
GENTLEMEN'S SINGLES CHAMPIONS

1877	S.W. Gore	*1907	N.E. Brookes	1947	J.A. Kramer	1977	B.R. Borg	2007	R. Federer
1878	P.F. Hadow	*1908	A.W. Gore	*1948	R. Falkenburg	1978	B.R. Borg	2008	R. Nadal
*1879	J.T. Hartley	1909	A.W. Gore	1949	F.R. Schroeder	1979	B.R. Borg	2009	R. Federer
1880	J.T. Hartley	1910	A.F. Wilding	*1950	J.E. Patty	1980	B.R. Borg	2010	R. Nadal
1881	W.C. Renshaw	1911	A.F. Wilding	1951	R. Savitt	1981	J.P. McEnroe	2011	N. Djokovic
1882	W.C. Renshaw	1912	A.F. Wilding	1952	F.A. Sedgman	1982	J.S. Connors	2012	R. Federer
1883	W.C. Renshaw	1913	A.F. Wilding	*1953	E.V. Seixas	1983	J.P. McEnroe	2013	A.B. Murray
1884	W.C. Renshaw	1914	N.E. Brookes	1954	J. Drobny	1984	J.P. McEnroe	2014	N. Djokovic
1885	W.C. Renshaw	1919	G.L. Patterson	1955	M.A. Trabert	1985	B.F. Becker	2015	N. Djokovic
1886	W.C. Renshaw	1920	W.T. Tilden	*1956	L.A. Hoad	1986	B.F. Becker	2016	A.B. Murray
*1887	H.F. Lawford	1921	W.T. Tilden	1957	L.A. Hoad	1987	P.H. Cash	2017	R. Federer
1888	J.E. Renshaw	**1922	G.L. Patterson	*1958	A.J. Cooper	1988	S.B. Edberg	2018	N. Djokovic
1889	W.C. Renshaw	*1923	W.M. Johnston	*1959	A.R. Olmedo	1989	B.F. Becker	2019	N. Djokovic
1890	W.J. Hamilton	*1924	J.R. Borotra	*1960	N.A. Fraser	1990	S.B. Edberg	2021	N. Djokovic
*1891	W. Baddeley	1925	J.R. Lacoste	1961	R.G. Laver	1991	M.D. Stich	2022	N. Djokovic
1892	W. Baddeley	*1926	J.R. Borotra	1962	R.G. Laver	1992	A.K. Agassi		
1893	J. Pim	1927	H.J. Cochet	*1963	C.R. McKinley	1993	P. Sampras		
1894	J. Pim	1928	J.R. Lacoste	1964	R.S. Emerson	1994	P. Sampras		
*1895	W. Baddeley	*1929	H.J. Cochet	1965	R.S. Emerson	1995	P. Sampras		
1896	H.S. Mahony	1930	W.T. Tilden	1966	M.M. Santana	1996	R.P.S. Krajicek		
1897	R.F. Doherty	*1931	S.B.B. Wood	1967	J.D. Newcombe	1997	P. Sampras		
1898	R.F. Doherty	1932	H.E. Vines	1968	R.G. Laver	1998	P. Sampras		
1899	R.F. Doherty	1933	J.H. Crawford	1969	R.G. Laver	1999	P. Sampras		
1900	R.F. Doherty	1934	F.J. Perry	1970	J.D. Newcombe	2000	P. Sampras		
1901	A.W. Gore	1935	F.J. Perry	1971	J.D. Newcombe	2001	G. Ivanisevic		
1902	H.L. Doherty	1936	F.J. Perry	*1972	S.R. Smith	2002	L.G. Hewitt		
1903	H.L. Doherty	*1937	J.D. Budge	*1973	J. Kodes	2003	R. Federer		
1904	H.L. Doherty	1938	J.D. Budge	1974	J.S. Connors	2004	R. Federer		
1905	H.L. Doherty	*1939	R.L. Riggs	1975	A.R. Ashe	2005	R. Federer		
1906	H.L. Doherty	*1946	Y.F.M. Petra	1976	B.R. Borg	2006	R. Federer		

For the years 1913, 1914 and 1919-1923 inclusive the above records include the "World's Championships on Grass" granted to The Lawn Tennis Association by The International Lawn Tennis Federation.

This title was then abolished and commencing in 1924 they became The Official Lawn Tennis Championships recognised by The International Lawn Tennis Federation.

Prior to 1922 the holders in the Singles Events and Gentlemen's Doubles did not compete in The Championships but met the winners of these events in the Challenge Rounds.

† Challenge Round abolished: holders subsequently played through.

* The holder did not defend the title.

LADIES' SINGLES CHAMPIONS

1884	M. Watson	*1913	D.K. Lambert Chambers	1952	M. Connolly	1982	M. Navratilova	2013	M. Bartoli
1885	M. Watson			1953	M. Connolly	1983	M. Navratilova	2014	P. Kvitova
1886	B. Bingley	1914	D.K. Lambert Chambers	1954	M. Connolly	1984	M. Navratilova	2015	S. Williams
1887	L. Dod			*1955	L. Brough	1985	M. Navratilova	2016	S. Williams
1888	L. Dod	1919	S. Lenglen	1956	S. Fry	1986	M. Navratilova	2017	G. Muguruza
*1889	B. Hillyard	1920	S. Lenglen	*1957	A. Gibson	1987	M. Navratilova	2018	A. Kerber
*1890	L. Rice	1921	S. Lenglen	1958	A. Gibson	1988	S. Graf	2019	S. Halep
*1891	L. Dod	†1922	S. Lenglen	*1959	M.E. Bueno	1989	S. Graf	*2021	A. Barty
1892	L. Dod	1923	S. Lenglen	1960	M.E. Bueno	1990	M. Navratilova	*2022	E. Rybakina
1893	L. Dod	1924	K. McKane	*1961	A. Mortimer	1991	S. Graf		
*1894	B. Hillyard	1925	S. Lenglen	1962	K. Susman	1992	S. Graf		
*1895	C. Cooper	1926	K. Godfree	*1963	M. Smith	1993	S. Graf		
1896	C. Cooper	1927	H. Wills	1964	M.E. Bueno	1994	C. Martinez		
1897	B. Hillyard	1928	H. Wills	1965	M. Smith	1995	S. Graf		
*1898	C. Cooper	1929	H. Wills	1966	B.J. King	1996	S. Graf		
1899	B. Hillyard	1930	H. Wills Moody	1967	B.J. King	*1997	M. Hingis		
1900	B. Hillyard	*1931	C. Aussem	1968	B.J. King	1998	J. Novotna		
1901	C. Sterry	*1932	H. Wills Moody	1969	A. Jones	1999	L. Davenport		
1902	M.E. Robb	1933	H. Wills Moody	*1970	M. Court	2000	V. Williams		
*1903	D.K. Douglass	*1934	D.E. Round	1971	E.F. Goolagong	2001	V. Williams		
1904	D.K. Douglass	1935	H. Wills Moody	1972	B.J. King	2002	S. Williams		
1905	M. Sutton	*1936	H.H. Jacobs	1973	B.J. King	2003	S. Williams		
1906	D.K. Douglass	1937	D.E. Round	1974	C.M. Evert	2004	M. Sharapova		
1907	M. Sutton	*1938	H. Wills Moody	1975	B.J. King	2005	V. Williams		
*1908	C. Sterry	*1939	A. Marble	*1976	C.M. Evert	2006	A. Mauresmo		
*1909	D.P. Boothby	*1946	P. Betz	1977	V. Wade	2007	V. Williams		
1910	D.K. Lambert Chambers	*1947	M. Osborne	1978	M. Navratilova	2008	V. Williams		
		1948	L. Brough	1979	M. Navratilova	2009	S. Williams		
1911	D.K. Lambert Chambers	1949	L. Brough	1980	E.F. Goolagong Cawley	2010	S. Williams		
		1950	L. Brough			2011	P. Kvitova		
*1912	E. Larcombe	1951	D. Hart	*1981	C.M. Evert Lloyd	2012	S. Williams		

GENTLEMEN'S DOUBLES CHAMPIONS

1884	E. Renshaw & W. Renshaw	1923	L.A. Godfree & R. Lycett	1965	J.D. Newcombe & A.D. Roche	1997	T.A. Woodbridge & M.R. Woodforde
1885	E. Renshaw & W. Renshaw	1924	F.T. Hunter & V. Richards	1966	K.N. Fletcher & J.D. Newcombe	1998	J. Eltingh & P. Haarhuis
1886	E. Renshaw & W. Renshaw	1925	J. Borotra & R. Lacoste	1967	R.A.J. Hewitt & F.D. McMillan	1999	M. Bhupathi & L. Paes
1887	P. Bowes-Lyon & H.W.W. Wilberforce	1926	J. Brugnon & H. Cochet	1968	J.D. Newcombe & A.D. Roche	2000	T.A. Woodbridge & M.R. Woodforde
1888	E. Renshaw & W. Renshaw	1927	F.T. Hunter & W.T. Tilden	1969	J.D. Newcombe & A.D. Roche	2001	D. Johnson & J. Palmer
1889	E. Renshaw & W. Renshaw	1928	J. Brugnon & H. Cochet	1970	J.D. Newcombe & A.D. Roche	2002	J. Bjorkman & T.A. Woodbridge
1890	J. Pim & F.O. Stoker	1929	W. Allison & J. Van Ryn	1971	R.S. Emerson & R.G. Laver		
1891	H. Baddeley & W. Baddeley	1930	W. Allison & J. Van Ryn	1972	R.A.J. Hewitt & F.D. McMillan	2003	J. Bjorkman & T.A. Woodbridge
1892	H.S. Barlow & E.W. Lewis	1931	G.M. Lott & J. Van Ryn	1973	J.S. Connors & I. Nastase		
1893	J. Pim & F.O. Stoker	1932	J. Borotra & J. Brugnon	1974	J.D. Newcombe & A.D. Roche	2004	J. Bjorkman & T.A. Woodbridge
1894	H. Baddeley & W. Baddeley	1933	J. Borotra & J. Brugnon	1975	V. Gerulaitis & A. Mayer		
1895	H. Baddeley & W. Baddeley	1934	G.M. Lott & L.R. Stoefen	1976	B.E. Gottfried & R. Ramirez	2005	S. Huss & W. Moodie
1896	H. Baddeley & W. Baddeley	1935	J.H. Crawford & A.K. Quist	1977	R.L. Case & G. Masters	2006	B. Bryan & M. Bryan
1897	H.L. Doherty & R.F. Doherty	1936	G.P. Hughes & C.R.D. Tuckey	1978	R.A.J. Hewitt & F.D. McMillan	2007	A. Clement & M. Llodra
1898	H.L. Doherty & R.F. Doherty	1937	J.D. Budge & G. Mako	1979	P. Fleming & J.P. McEnroe	2008	D. Nestor & N. Zimonjić
1899	H.L. Doherty & R.F. Doherty	1938	J.D. Budge & G. Mako	1980	P. McNamara & P. McNamee	2009	D. Nestor & N. Zimonjić
1900	H.L. Doherty & R.F. Doherty	1939	R.L. Riggs & E.T. Cooke	1981	P. Fleming & J.P. McEnroe	2010	J. Melzer & P. Petzschner
1901	H.L. Doherty & R.F. Dohe rty	1946	T. Brown & J. Kramer	1982	P. McNamara & P. McNamee	2011	B. Bryan & M. Bryan
1902	F.L. Riseley & S.H. Smith	1947	R. Falkenburg & J. Kramer	1983	P. Fleming & J.P. McEnroe	2012	J. Marray & F. Nielsen
1903	H.L. Doherty & R.F. Doherty	1948	J.E. Bromwich & F.A. Sedgman	1984	P. Fleming & J.P. McEnroe	2013	B. Bryan & M. Bryan
1904	H.L. Doherty & R.F. Doherty	1949	R. Gonzales & F. Parker	1985	H.P. Guenthardt & B. Taroczy	2014	V. Pospisil & J.E. Sock
1905	H.L. Doherty & R.F. Doherty	1950	J.E. Bromwich & A.K. Quist	1986	J. Nystrom & M. Wilander	2015	J-J. Rojer & H. Tecau
1906	F.L. Riseley & S.H. Smith	1951	K. McGregor & F.A. Sedgman	1987	K. Flach & R. Seguso	2016	P-H. Herbert & N. Mahut
1907	N.E. Brookes & A.F. Wilding	1952	K. McGregor & F.A. Sedgman	1988	K. Flach & R. Seguso	2017	L. Kubot & M. Melo
1908	A.F. Wilding & M.J.G. Ritchie	1953	L.A. Hoad & K.R. Rosewall	1989	J.B. Fitzgerald & A. Jarryd	2018	M. Bryan & J. Sock
1909	A.W. Gore & H. Roper Barrett	1954	R.N. Hartwig & M.G. Rose	1990	R. Leach & J. Pugh	2019	J.S. Cabal & R. Farah
1910	A.F. Wilding & M.J.G. Ritchie	1955	R.N. Hartwig & L.A. Hoad	1991	J.B. Fitzgerald & A. Jarryd	2021	N. Mektic & M. Pavic
1911	M. Decugis & A.H. Gobert	1956	L.A. Hoad & K.R. Rosewall	1992	J.P. McEnroe & M. Stich	2022	M. Ebden & M. Purcell
1912	H. Roper Barrett & C.P. Dixon	1957	G. Mulloy & B. Patty	1993	T.A. Woodbridge & M.R. Woodforde		
1913	H. Roper Barrett & C.P. Dixon	1958	S. Davidson & U. Schmidt				
1914	N.E. Brookes & A.F. Wilding	1959	R. Emerson & N.A. Fraser	1994	T.A. Woodbridge & M.R. Woodforde		
1919	R.V. Thomas & P. O'Hara-Wood	1960	R.H. Osuna & R.D. Ralston				
1920	C.S. Garland & R.N. Williams	1961	R. Emerson & N.A. Fraser	1995	T.A. Woodbridge & M.R. Woodforde		
1921	R. Lycett & M. Woosnam	1962	R.A.J. Hewitt & F.S. Stolle				
1922	J.O. Anderson & R. Lycett	1963	R.H. Osuna & A. Palafox	1996	T.A. Woodbridge & M.R. Woodforde		
		1964	R.A.J. Hewitt & F.S. Stolle				

LADIES' DOUBLES CHAMPIONS

1913	D.P. Boothby & W. McNair	1955	A. Mortimer & J.A. Shilcock	1987	C. Kohde-Kilsch & H. Sukova	2021	S-W. Hsieh & E. Mertens
1914	A.M. Morton & E. Ryan	1956	A. Buxton & A. Gibson	1988	S. Graf & G. Sabatini	2022	B. Krejcikova & K. Siniakova
1919	S. Lenglen & E. Ryan	1957	A. Gibson & D.R. Hard	1989	J. Novotna & H. Sukova		
1920	S. Lenglen & E. Ryan	1958	M.E. Bueno & A. Gibson	1990	J. Novotna & H. Sukova		
1921	S. Lenglen & E. Ryan	1959	J. Arth & D.R. Hard	1991	L. Savchenko & N. Zvereva		
1922	S. Lenglen & E. Ryan	1960	M.E. Bueno & D.R. Hard	1992	G. Fernandez & N. Zvereva		
1923	S. Lenglen & E. Ryan	1961	K. Hantze & B.J. Moffitt	1993	G. Fernandez & N. Zvereva		
1924	H. Wightman & H. Wills	1962	B.J. Moffitt & K. Susman	1994	G. Fernandez & N. Zvereva		
1925	S. Lenglen & E. Ryan	1963	M.E. Bueno & D.R. Hard	1995	J. Novotna & A. Sanchez Vicario		
1926	M.K. Browne & E. Ryan	1964	M. Smith & L.R. Turner				
1927	E. Ryan & H. Wills	1965	M.E. Bueno & B.J. Moffitt	1996	M. Hingis & H. Sukova		
1928	P. Holcroft-Watson & P. Saunders	1966	M.E. Bueno & N. Richey	1997	G. Fernandez & N. Zvereva		
		1967	R. Casals & B.J. King	1998	M. Hingis & J. Novotna		
1929	P. Holcroft-Watson & P. Michell	1968	R. Casals & B.J. King	1999	L. Davenport & C. Morariu		
1930	H. Wills Moody & E. Ryan	1969	M. Court & J.A.M. Tegart	2000	S. Williams & V. Williams		
1931	P. Mudford & D. Shepherd-Barron	1970	R. Casals & B.J. King	2001	L.M. Raymond & R.P. Stubbs		
		1971	R. Casals & B.J. King	2002	S. Williams & V. Williams		
1932	D. Metaxa & J. Sigart	1972	B.J. King & B.F. Stove	2003	K. Clijsters & A. Sugiyama		
1933	S. Mathieu & E. Ryan	1973	R. Casals & B.J. King	2004	C. Black & R.P. Stubbs		
1934	S. Mathieu & E. Ryan	1974	E.F. Goolagong & M. Michel	2005	C. Black & L. Huber		
1935	F. James & K.E. Stammers	1975	A.K. Kiyomura & K. Sawamatsu	2006	Z. Yan & J. Zheng		
1936	F. James & K.E. Stammers	1976	C.M. Evert & M. Navratilova	2007	C. Black & L. Huber		
1937	S. Mathieu & B. Yorke	1977	H.F. Gourlay Cawley & J.C. Russell	2008	S. Williams & V. Williams		
1938	S.P. Fabyan & A. Marble			2009	S. Williams & V. Williams		
1939	S.P. Fabyan & A. Marble	1978	K. Melville Reid & W.M. Turnbull	2010	V. King & Y. Shvedova		
1946	L. Brough & M. Osborne			2011	K. Peschke & K. Srebotnik		
1947	D. Hart & P.C. Todd	1979	B.J. King & M. Navratilova	2012	S. Williams & V. Williams		
1948	L. Brough & M. du Pont	1980	K. Jordan & A.E. Smith	2013	S-W. Hsieh & S. Peng		
1949	L. Brough & M. du Pont	1981	M. Navratilova & P.H. Shriver	2014	S. Errani & R. Vinci		
1950	L. Brough & M. du Pont	1982	M. Navratilova & P.H. Shriver	2015	M. Hingis & S. Mirza		
1951	S. Fry & D. Hart	1983	M. Navratilova & P.H. Shriver	2016	S. Williams & V. Williams		
1952	S. Fry & D. Hart	1984	M. Navratilova & P.H. Shriver	2017	E. Makarova & E. Vesnina		
1953	S. Fry & D. Hart	1985	K. Jordan & E. Smylie	2018	B. Krejcikova & K. Siniakova		
1954	L. Brough & M. du Pont	1986	M. Navratilova & P.H. Shriver	2019	S-W. Hsieh & B. Strycova		

MIXED DOUBLES CHAMPIONS

1913	H. Crisp & A. Tuckey	1950	E.W. Sturgess & L. Brough	1978	F.D. McMillan & B.F. Stove	2004	W. Black & C. Black
1914	J.C. Parke & E. Larcombe	1951	F.A. Sedgman & D. Hart	1979	R.A.J. Hewitt & G.R. Stevens	2005	M. Bhupathi & M. Pierce
1919	R. Lycett & E. Ryan	1952	F.A. Sedgman & D. Hart	1980	J.R. Austin & T. Austin	2006	A. Ram & V. Zvonareva
1920	G.L. Patterson & S. Lenglen	1953	V. Seixas & D. Hart	1981	F.D. McMillan & B.F. Stove	2007	J. Murray & J. Jankovic
1921	R. Lycett & E. Ryan	1954	V. Seixas & D. Hart	1982	K. Curren & A.E. Smith	2008	B. Bryan & S. Stosur
1922	P. O'Hara-Wood & S. Lenglen	1955	V. Seixas & S. Fry	1983	J.M. Lloyd & W.M. Turnbull	2009	M. Knowles & A-L. Groenefeld
1923	R. Lycett & E. Ryan	1956	V. Seixas & S. Fry	1984	J.M. Lloyd & W.M. Turnbull	2010	L. Paes & C. Black
1924	J.B. Gilbert & K. McKane	1957	M.G. Rose & D.R. Hard	1985	P. McNamee & M. Navratilova	2011	J. Melzer & I. Benesova
1925	J. Borotra & S. Lenglen	1958	R.N. Howe & L. Coghlan	1986	K. Flach & K. Jordan	2012	M. Bryan & L.M. Raymond
1926	L.A. Godfree & K. Godfree	1959	R. Laver & D.R. Hard	1987	M.J. Bates & J.M. Durie	2013	D. Nestor & K. Mladenovic
1927	F.T. Hunter & E. Ryan	1960	R. Laver & D.R. Hard	1988	S.E. Stewart & Z.L. Garrison	2014	N. Zimonjic & S. Stosur
1928	P.D.B. Spence & E. Ryan	1961	F.S. Stolle & L.R. Turner	1989	J. Pugh & J. Novotna	2015	L. Paes & M. Hingis
1929	F.T. Hunter & H. Wills	1962	N.A. Fraser & M. du Pont	1990	R. Leach & Z.L. Garrison	2016	H. Kontinen & H. Watson
1930	J.H. Crawford & E. Ryan	1963	K.N. Fletcher & M. Smith	1991	J.B. Fitzgerald & E. Smylie	2017	J. Murray & M. Hingis
1931	G.M. Lott & A. Harper	1964	F.S. Stolle & L.R. Turner	1992	C. Suk &	2018	A. Peya & N. Melichar
1932	E. Maier & E. Ryan	1965	K.N. Fletcher & M. Smith		L. Savchenko-Neiland	2019	I. Dodig & L. Chan
1933	G. von Cramm &	1966	K.N. Fletcher & M. Smith	1993	M. Woodforde &	2021	N. Skupski & D. Krawczyk
	H. Krahwinkel	1967	O.K. Davidson & B.J. King		M. Navratilova	2022	N. Skupski & D. Krawczyk
1934	R. Miki & D.E. Round	1968	K.N. Fletcher & M. Court	1994	T.A. Woodbridge & H. Sukova		
1935	F.J. Perry & D.E. Round	1969	F.S. Stolle & A. Jones	1995	J. Stark & M. Navratilova		
1936	F.J. Perry & D.E. Round	1970	I. Nastase & R. Casals	1996	C. Suk & H. Sukova		
1937	J.D. Budge & A. Marble	1971	O.K. Davidson & B.J. King	1997	C. Suk & H. Sukova		
1938	J.D. Budge & A. Marble	1972	I. Nastase & Miss R. Casals	1998	M. Mirnyi & S. Williams		
1939	R.L. Riggs & A. Marble	1973	O.K. Davidson & B.J. King	1999	L. Paes & L.M. Raymond		
1946	T. Brown & L. Brough	1974	O.K. Davidson & B.J. King	2000	D. Johnson & K. Po		
1947	J.E. Bromwich & L. Brough	1975	M.C. Riessen & M. Court	2001	L. Friedl & D. Hantuchova		
1948	J.E. Bromwich & L. Brough	1976	A.D. Roche & F. Durr	2002	M. Bhupathi & E. Likhovtseva		
1949	E.W. Sturgess & S.P. Summers	1977	R.A.J. Hewitt & G.R. Stevens	2003	L. Paes & M. Navratilova		

GENTLEMEN'S WHEELCHAIR SINGLES CHAMPIONS

2016	G. Reid	2018	S. Olsson	2021	J. Gerard
2017	S. Olsson	2019	G. Fernandez	2022	S. Kunieda

GENTLEMEN'S WHEELCHAIR DOUBLES CHAMPIONS

2005	M. Jeremiasz & J. Mistry	2011	M. Scheffers & R. Vink	2017	A. Hewett & G. Reid
2006	S. Kunieda & S. Saida	2012	T. Egberink & M. Jeremiasz	2018	A. Hewett & G. Reid
2007	R. Ammerlaan & R. Vink	2013	S. Houdet & S. Kunieda	2019	J. Gerard & S. Olsson
2008	R. Ammerlaan & R. Vink	2014	S. Houdet & S. Kunieda	2021	A. Hewett & G. Reid
2009	S. Houdet & M. Jeremiasz	2015	G. Fernandez & N. Peifer	2022	G. Fernandez & S. Kunieda
2010	R. Ammerlaan & S. Olsson	2016	A. Hewett & G. Reid		

LADIES' WHEELCHAIR SINGLES CHAMPIONS

2016	J. Griffioen	2018	D. de Groot	2021	D. de Groot
2017	D. de Groot	2019	A. van Koot	2022	D. de Groot

LADIES' WHEELCHAIR DOUBLES CHAMPIONS

2009	K. Homan & E. Vergeer	2013	J. Griffioen & A. van Koot	2017	Y. Kamiji & J. Whiley	2022	Y. Kamiji & D. Mathewson
2010	E. Vergeer & S. Walraven	2014	Y. Kamiji & J. Whiley	2018	D. de Groot & Y. Kamiji		
2011	E. Vergeer & S. Walraven	2015	Y. Kamiji & J. Whiley	2019	D. de Groot & A. van Koot		
2012	J. Griffioen & A. van Koot	2016	Y. Kamiji & J. Whiley	2021	Y. Kamiji & J. Whiley		

QUAD WHEELCHAIR SINGLES CHAMPIONS

2019	D. Alcott	2021	D. Alcott	2022	S. Schroder

QUAD WHEELCHAIR DOUBLES CHAMPIONS

2019	D. Alcott & A. Lapthorne	2021	A. Lapthorne & D. Wagner	2022	S. Schroder & N. Vink

18&U BOYS' SINGLES CHAMPIONS

1947	K. Nielsen	1963	N. Kalogeropoulos	1979	R. Krishnan	1995	O. Mutis	2011	L. Saville
1948	S.O. Stockenberg	1964	I. El Shafei	1980	T. Tulasne	1996	V. Voltchkov	2012	F. Peliwo
1949	S.O. Stockenberg	1965	V. Korotkov	1981	M.W. Anger	1997	W. Whitehouse	2013	G. Quinzi
1950	J.A.T. Horn	1966	V. Korotkov	1982	P.H. Cash	1998	R. Federer	2014	N. Rubin
1951	J. Kupferburger	1967	M. Orantes	1983	S.B. Edberg	1999	J. Melzer	2015	R. Opelka
1952	R.K. Wilson	1968	J.G. Alexander	1984	M. Kratzmann	2000	N.P.A. Mahut	2016	D. Shapovalov
1953	W.A. Knight	1969	B.M. Bertram	1985	L. Lavalle	2001	R. Valent	2017	A. Davidovich Fokina
1954	R. Krishnan	1970	B.M. Bertram	1986	E. Velez	2002	T.C. Reid	2018	C.H. Tseng
1955	M.P. Hann	1971	R.I. Kreiss	1987	D. Nargiso	2003	F. Mergea	2019	S. Mochizuki
1956	R.E. Holmberg	1972	B.R. Borg	1988	N. Pereira	2004	G. Monfils	2021	S. Banerjee
1957	J.I. Tattersall	1973	W.W. Martin	1989	L.J.N. Kulti	2005	J. Chardy	2022	M. Poljicak
1958	E.H. Buchholz	1974	W.W. Martin	1990	L.A. Paes	2006	T. De Bakker		
1959	T. Lejus	1975	C.J. Lewis	1991	K.J.T. Enqvist	2007	D. Young		
1960	A.R. Mandelstam	1976	H.P. Guenthardt	1992	D. Skoch	2008	G. Dimitrov		
1961	C.E. Graebner	1977	V.A.W. Winitsky	1993	R. Sabau	2009	A. Kuznetsov		
1962	S.J. Matthews	1978	I. Lendl	1994	S.M. Humphries	2010	M. Fucsovics		

18&U BOYS' DOUBLES CHAMPIONS

1982	P.H. Cash & J. Frawley	1992	S. Baldas & S. Draper	2004	B. Evans & S. Oudsema	2016	K. Raisma & S. Tsitsipas
1983	M. Kratzmann & S. Youl	1993	S. Downs & J. Greenhalgh	2005	J. Levine & M. Shabaz	2017	A. Geller & Y.H. Hsu
1984	R. Brown & R.V. Weiss	1994	B. Ellwood & M.A. Philippoussis	2006	K. Damico & N. Schnugg	2018	Y. Erel & O. Virtanen
1985	A. Moreno & J. Yzaga	1995	M. Lee & J.M. Trotman	2007	D. Lopez & M. Trevisan	2019	J. Forejtek & J. Lehecka
1986	T. Carbonell & P. Korda	1996	D. Bracciali & J. Robichaud	2008	C-P. Hsieh & T-H. Yang	2021	E. Butvilas &
1987	J.R. Stoltenberg &	1997	L. Horna & N. Massu	2009	P-H. Herbert & K. Krawietz		A. Manzanera Pertusa
	T.A. Woodbridge	1998	R. Federer & O.L.P. Rochus	2010	L. Broady & T. Farquharson	2022	S. Gorzny & A. Michelsen
1988	J.R. Stoltenberg &	1999	G. Coria & D. Nalbandian	2011	G. Morgan & M. Pavic		
	T.A. Woodbridge	2000	D. Coene & K. Vliegen	2012	A. Harris & N. Kyrgios		
1989	J.E. Palmer & J.A. Stark	2001	F. Dancevic & G. Lapentti	2013	T. Kokkinakis & N. Kyrgios		
1990	S. Lareau & S. Leblanc	2002	F. Mergea & H. Tecau	2014	O. Luz & M. Zormann		
1991	K. Alami & G. Rusedski	2003	F. Mergea & H. Tecau	2015	N-H. Ly & S. Nagal		

18&U GIRLS' SINGLES CHAMPIONS

1947	G. Domken	1963	D.M. Salfati	1979	M.L. Piatek	1995	A. Olsza	2011	A. Barty
1948	O. Miskova	1964	J.M. Bartkowicz	1980	D. Freeman	1996	A. Mauresmo	2012	E. Bouchard
1949	C. Mercelis	1965	O.V. Morozova	1981	Z.L. Garrison	1997	C.C. Black	2013	B. Bencic
1950	L.M. Cornell	1966	B. Lindstrom	1982	C. Tanvier	1998	K. Srebotnik	2014	J. Ostapenko
1951	L.M. Cornell	1967	J.H. Salmone	1983	P. Paradis	1999	I. Tulyaganova	2015	S. Zhuk
1952	F. J. I. ten Bosch	1968	K.S. Pigeon	1984	A.N. Croft	2000	M.E. Salerni	2016	A. Potapova
1953	D. Kilian	1969	K. Sawamatsu	1985	A. Holikova	2001	A. Widjaja	2017	C. Liu
1954	V.A. Pitt	1970	S.A. Walsh	1986	N.M. Zvereva	2002	V. Douchevina	2018	I. Swiatek
1955	S.M. Armstrong	1971	M.V. Kroshina	1987	N.M. Zvereva	2003	K. Flipkens	2019	D. Snigur
1956	A.S. Haydon	1972	I.S. Kloss	1988	B.A.N. Schultz	2004	K. Bondarenko	2021	A. Mintegi Del Olmo
1957	M.G. Arnold	1973	A.K. Kiyomura	1989	A. Strnadova	2005	A.R. Radwanska	2022	L. Hovde
1958	S.M. Moore	1974	M. Jausovec	1990	A. Strnadova	2006	C. Wozniacki		
1959	J. Cross	1975	N.Y. Chmyreva	1991	B. Rittner	2007	U. Radwanska		
1960	K.J. Hantze	1976	N.Y. Chmyreva	1992	C.R. Rubin	2008	L.M.D. Robson		
1961	G. Baksheeva	1977	L. Antonoplis	1993	N. Feber	2009	N. Lertcheewakarn		
1962	G. Baksheeva	1978	T.A. Austin	1994	M. Hingis	2010	K. Pliskova		

18&U GIRLS' DOUBLES CHAMPIONS

1982	E.A. Herr & P. Barg	1994	E. De Villiers & E.E. Jelfs	2005	V.A. Azarenka & A. Szavay	2015	D. Galfi & F. Stollar
1983	P.A. Fendick & P. Hy	1995	C.C. Black & A. Olsza	2006	A. Kleybanova &	2016	U.M. Arconada & C. Liu
1984	C. Kuhlman & S.C. Rehe	1996	O. Barabanschikova &		A. Pavlyuchenkova	2017	O. Danilovic & K. Juvan
1985	L. Field & J.G. Thompson		A. Mauresmo	2007	A. Pavlyuchenkova &	2018	X.Wang & X. Wang
1986	M. Jaggard & L. O'Neill	1997	C.C. Black & I. Selyutina		U. Radwanska	2019	S. Broadus & A. Forbes
1987	N. Medvedeva & N.M. Zvereva	1998	E. Dyrberg & J. Kostanic	2008	P. Hercog & J. Moore	2021	K. Dmitruk & D. Shnaider
1988	J.A. Faull & R. McQuillan	1999	D. Bedanova & M.E. Salerni	2009	N. Lertcheewakarn & S. Peers	2022	R. Nijkamp & A. Okutoyi
1989	J.M. Capriati & M.J. McGrath	2000	I. Gaspar & T. Perebiynis	2010	T. Babos & S. Stephens		
1990	K. Habsudova & A. Strnadova	2001	G. Dulko & A. Harkleroad	2011	E. Bouchard & G. Min		
1991	C. Barclay & L. Zaltz	2002	E. Clijsters & B. Strycova	2012	E. Bouchard & T. Townsend		
1992	M. Avotins & L. McShea	2003	A. Kleybanova & S. Mirza	2013	B. Krejcikova & K. Siniakova		
1993	L. Courtois & N. Feber	2004	V.A. Azarenka & V. Havartsova	2014	T. Grende and Q.Y. Ye		

14&U BOYS' SINGLES CHAMPIONS

2022	S. Cho

14&U GIRLS' SINGLES CHAMPIONS

2022	A. Tatu

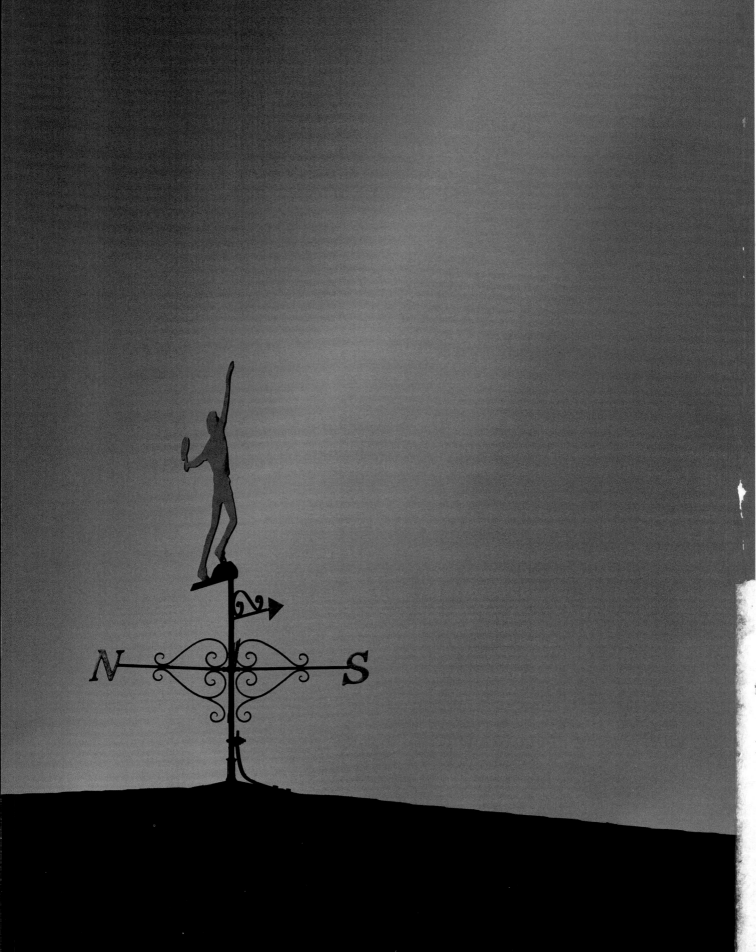